THE CANDLES SHE LIT

For

Mervin & Irene

Rosenberg –

All the Best!

Stella K. Hershan

Val-Kill, Nov. 16/01

THE CANDLES SHE LIT
THE LEGACY OF
ELEANOR ROOSEVELT

Stella K. Hershan

Published by
Eleanor Roosevelt Center at Val-Kill, ERVK   Hyde Park, New York

For my children,

Lisa and Allan
and their children,
Sheryl and Larry
and my great-grandchildren,
Jylian Eman
Dilyn Reese
Sydnie Elana

and

in memory
of
Selma Fromkin

"She would rather light candles than curse the darkness and her glow has warmed the world."

These words were spoken by U.N. Ambassador Adlai E. Stevenson after the death of Eleanor Roosevelt on November 7, 1962.

The Candles She Lit brings to the reader for the first time untold stories of people whose lives had been dramatically changed sometimes even saved by the solace and practical aid of Eleanor Roosevelt. She was a woman of the people. Her life is a shining example of the difference one person can make, an extraordinary picture of a woman's service to mankind. As First Lady and during the long years after the White House, Mrs. Roosevelt worked untiringly to enhance the welfare and dignity of people everywhere. Every appeal for help was answered, every letter of the hundreds she received daily got a reply. Everyone who came into her orbit, whether they were kings or servants, were treated with the same warmth and courteousness. Yet, she was not a paragon of virtue; she could get angry, she could laugh, mostly at herself, and she suffered a great deal.

The Candles She Lit is both a brief biography of Eleanor Roosevelt and a testimony to the positive and influential effect she had on others. Youth, family, young adulthood and her marriage to Franklin, the White House period, and the years alone are richly portrayed. The picture that emerges is of an idealistic, intelligent, honest, and compassionate woman always ready to reach out to those in need. The role of Eleanor Roosevelt in the drafting of "The Declaration of Human Rights" is also pointed out. She considered the Declaration her "crowning achievement" because it encompasses every human being on our planet.

Stella K. Hershan draws on the testimony of numerous people from all walks of life. Anecdotes, stories, and memories of members of her staff, school children, college students, survivors of the Holocaust, the famous and the not famous, provide a loving testimonial to the memory of one of the greatest women of the twentieth century.

The Story of Val-Kill

"The greatest thing I have learned is how good it is to come home again," Eleanor Roosevelt told a friend in the late 1950's. She was referring to a beautiful, tranquil spot called Val-Kill on FDR's estate which provided her with a retreat and later a home during the most productive years of her life, 1926-62. Finally after years of living in the homes of others - grandmother, mother-in-law, rentals - she had a place of her own where she could live and entertain as she pleased.

Val-Kill quickly became the social center for the Roosevelt family in Hyde Park. Throughout the early years, the site was often a gathering place for numerous political personages who came to Hyde Park to see the President. Visitors included Winston Churchill, King George and Queen Elizabeth of England, Queen Wilhemina and Crown Princess Julianna of the Netherlands and other European heads of state. American leaders in political, economic, labor and cultural life attended functions at Val-Kill.

Mrs. Roosevelt's time at Val-Kill was limited by the scope of her outside activities. (She did keep an apartment and office in New York City, but considered her Hyde Park cottage her real home.) Between 1946 and 1952, when she served as a U.S. delegate to the United Nations, many of her fellow delegates and other UN employees were entertained at Val-Kill. Later she became the key figure in the American Association for the United Nations and often invited members to Hyde Park. Her role as a major influence in the Democratic Party grew throughout the fifties, and many prominent politicians came to Val-Kill seeking her counsel and support. Adlai Stevenson was a frequent visitor, and John F. Kennedy came in 1960 wooing her support for his campaign for the presidency.

After FDR's death, many world leaders made trips to Hyde Park when they visited this country to see his grave and to talk with Eleanor Roosevelt. Among those who came were Soviet leader Nikita Khrushchev, Marshall Tito of Yugoslavia, Emperor Haile Selassie of Ethiopia and Prime Minister Nehru of India. From time to time, groups of college students came to Val-Kill to talk to Eleanor Roosevelt about a variety of subjects. Each summer she entertained over 150 boys from the Wiltwyck School for troubled youths, which was located across the river from Hyde Park. She served them hot dogs, planned games for them, and read to them, often from Kipling. In spite of the steady procession of family and guests at Val-Kill, the site remained Eleanor's sanctuary, the place where she could go to rest, to seek inspiration and self-renewal. Of all the places she had lived in her life, Val-Kill was the only one she could call home.

On November 7, 1962, Eleanor Roosevelt died. In 1976, a local group with some state figures as well as Roosevelt family members was formed to save Val-Kill from developers. Their efforts sparked interest in and drew support from national, congressional and Senate leaders for creating a national historic site for this great woman. In May 1977, President Carter signed the bill creating the Eleanor Roosevelt National Historic Site, "in order to commemorate for the education, inspiration, and benefit of present and future generations the life work of an outstanding woman in American history." It is the only such site dedicated to a First Lady. That local group became the Eleanor Roosevelt Center at Val-kill (ERVK) which operates from the site under a unique agreement with the National Park Service.

All proceeds from the sale of this book go to the Eleanor Roosevelt Center at Val-Kill. The Center is dedicated to preserving Mrs. Roosevelt's home as a living memorial and a center for dialogue and change through programs related to her humanitarian concerns.

(For more information, visit our website: http://www.ervk.org)

Your Support is Needed!

Make a donation to further Eleanor Roosevelt's commitment to Human Rights. The Eleanor Roosevelt Center at Val-Kill relies on private donations as the major source of support for our work and programs that include: an innovative Girls' Leadership Workshop that promotes leadership development for high school girls from diverse backgrounds, Community Programs initiative that consists of Welfare Reform and Human Rights Monitoring and Diversity in the Workplace, a Teacher's Workshop on Human Rights, a Human Rights Lecture Series and Elderhostel programs.

We encourage you to consider a gift in one of our special categories

First Lady's Club	$10,000 or more
ER Fellowship	$ 5,000 - $9,999
ERVK Partnership	$ 2,500 - $4,999
Eleanor Roosevelt Society	$ 1,000 - $2,499
Val-Kill Circle	$ 500 - $ 999
Stone Cottage Member	$ 100 - $ 499

Federal Employees may donate to ERVK through the Combined Federal Campaign

Inquiries can be addressed to:

Eleanor Roosevelt Center at Val-Kill
PO Box 255
Hyde Park, NY 12538

Contents

Photo essay follows page 61.

Foreword

My grandmother, Eleanor Roosevelt, died when I was in my early ado-
lescence. She was enough of a presence in my life, however, for me to
be able to describe a little of what she was like.

We lived quite near her in Hyde Park, New York, so we spent all of
the major holidays and a good many summer days with her at the house
she called Val-Kill. She made a great effort to be with her grandchildren, maybe because she had not had the time to spend with her own
children when they were growing up in the White House. She had a
quiet but firm way about her, and I remember a way she had of looking
at you when you had said something she did not necessarily approve of.
She was very tolerant, however, of my very self-absorbed behavior. She
also had a rather lilting, sing-song voice that was uniquely hers.

Looking back on it now, I see my relationship with her as a wasted
opportunity; a typically adult viewpoint! You see, I never fully compre-
hended the fact that she was different from other grandmothers. I knew
that she was famous and that people fussed over her, but I had several
famous family members and was used to that. To a child, being famous
is not particularly impressive unless one is famous for something important to children. What was impressive, to me, about my grandmother
was the fact that she allowed her grandchildren to eat with the grown-
ups; that she talked to me often; that she brought me trinkets from her
travels; and when we went to Val-Kill for Christmas there were mounds
of presents! I once completely disgraced myself and my mother by looking at my pile of presents and asking in a loud voice, "Is that all?" My

grandmother ignored this horrible remark, but my mother did not! I loved swimming in her pool in the summer and being at her picnics. There were always different people around who I'm sure would have been fascinating if only I'd been older.

My grandmother was loved by her extended family and friends, who were drawn to her and the relaxed, warm, and cozy atmosphere she created at Val-Kill. When I read Ms. Hershan's wonderful book about her I brought to it memories of a kind, wise grandmother who did not reprimand me when I was rude or tell me to stop running up and down the stairs with my cousins. She was certainly a multi-faceted and multi-talented woman who was capable of success in many roles. I hope this book will give you a lively and vivid impression of her as a girl, a wife, a career-woman, and that I have been able to describe her in her role as grandmother.

Nancy Roosevelt Ireland

Preface

Working on this book was like walking around with a magic wand. "I am collecting stories about Mrs. Eleanor Roosevelt," I would tell people. Men, women, old people, young people, chance acquaintances I met on a bus, at a party, a lecture, in libraries, anywhere—all would react with the sudden spark of a smile, a warm glow.

"She was extraordinary," people said, "so kind. She cared so much, about everyone." "She is a role model for us," said the young women. "She stood up for herself. She was independent. And yet she supported her husband in his work."

"She gave the commencement address at my school," an older woman said. "I will never forget her. The kids made fun of her at first—her clothes, her high-pitched voice. But they all fell silent very soon. They listened. They really listened. And afterward everyone crowded close, for a glimpse of her eyes, a firm handshake. She asked me my name! And she really sounded as though she was glad to meet me. She even repeated my name."

"As a young girl I worked in a summer camp near Poughkeepsie," said Adelaide, a lady seated next to me at a museum film. "A few of the counselors went to see a movie in town. It was *Goodbye, Mr. Chips.* Suddenly we heard someone chuckle behind us. We turned around. 'Oh, my God! It's Mrs. Roosevelt!' we whispered. The wife of the president! We almost fainted. She smiled at us, said, 'Hello.' We could barely talk. But she wanted to hear what we young people thought about the movie."

And so it went. Through the magic name of Eleanor Roosevelt, the world opened up to me. And I found that the candles she lit during her lifetime are still burning everywhere.

I wish I could name each and every individual who gave me an "Eleanor Roosevelt story" and thus made this book possible. But since there were so very many who remembered Mrs. Roosevelt and who took the trouble to share their memories with me, all I can do is to thank them most sincerely for their generosity. My special thanks, however, go out to a young college student at Furman University, Lalie Chambers, whose active help and great enthusiasm upon finding a new role model in Mrs. Roosevelt gave me the courage to write yet another book about "Eleanor." I also extend my very warm gratitude, for the endless patience and unstinting help with the research that made this book possible, to all the wonderful park rangers in Hyde Park, New York, who have become my friends.

Part I _____

A Brief Biography

Chapter 1 ──────────────────

Youth

The image of ourselves that our parents give us when we are small remains with us throughout our lives. Anna Eleanor Roosevelt was told that she was homely.

She was born on October 11, 1884, at 11 West 37th Street in New York City. Her mother was Anna Hall Roosevelt, a woman of great beauty. People kept reminding the little girl that she did not at all resemble her mother. Once she was stamped as unattractive, everyone tended to overlook the extraordinary intelligent, blue eyes, the sensitive little face, the glossy, long chestnut hair. Eleanor, they said, was "plain," and everyone believed it—most of all, Eleanor herself. Her father was Elliott Roosevelt, a man whom women—including his young daughter—found irresistible. Yet even his great affection for her could not make the child feel that she was anything but plain. Only someone who has felt this stigma can really understand what it means. That inner sadness and hopelessness make one avoid any mirror, worse still a photograph of oneself. Someone who is plain is always starved for affection and must work very hard to win people's approval. Love, when it comes, seems undeserved, and the tragedies of life appear to be a justified punishment.

"Attention and admiration were things through all of my childhood which I wanted because I was made to feel so conscious of the fact that nothing about me would attract attention or bring me admiration," Eleanor Roosevelt said in her autobiography.

In my family everyone was a great social success, especially the women. A woman with the background we grew up in was educated in order to be a success in society. You learned languages, if you were fortunate enough to be able to play the piano or sing a little bit, that was pleasant. But everything you did was so that you would grace society. To be a beautiful woman would be an enormous asset, and all of my mother's family were beautiful, and so it was a shock to the family when I was just a very ordinary looking little girl.[1]

The Roosevelts and the Halls were both socially prominent. The Roosevelts were a wealthy family of Dutch descent, and Elliott, Eleanor's father, was the younger brother of Theodore, who became twenty-sixth president of the United States (1901–09). A known sportsman and big-game hunter, Elliott was seldom with his family. He also had a severe problem—alcoholism. The Halls were from the same family as Philip Livingston, a signer of the Declaration of Independence of English descent.

When Eleanor was five years old, a baby brother, Elliott, was born. Two years later, a second brother, Hall, made his appearance. How did Eleanor feel about the births of her siblings? In her autobiography, she does not say much.

My little brother Ellie adored my mother and he was so good he never had to be reproved. The baby Hall was always called Josh and was too small to do anything but sit upon her lap contentedly. I felt a curious barrier between myself and them. I still can remember standing at the door, often with my finger in my mouth, and I can see the look in my mother's eyes and hear the tone of her voice as she said: "Come in, Granny." If a visitor was there she might turn and say, "She is such a funny child, so old-fashioned that we always call her Granny." I wanted to sink through the floor in shame.[2]

In 1892, when Eleanor was just eight years old, her mother died of diphtheria. "Death meant nothing to me," she wrote in her autobiography about her mother's death. (Brother Elliott would die a year later of scarlet fever.) "One thing wiped out everything else. My father was coming back and I would see him soon!"[3]

Elliott Roosevelt did come back, sporadically, so it was Mrs. V. G. Hall, Eleanor's grandmother, who took the three children into her home, an old-fashioned brownstone on West Thirty-seventh Street. The grandfather had died long before, but two young aunts and two uncles were still living at home. The staff consisted of a butler, a cook, a housemaid, and a laundress. The drawing room had massive gilt furniture upholstered in blue damask, and in a wide bow window in the library stood a piano.

"Never by word or deed did any of the family make us feel that we were not in our own home," wrote Eleanor. "Life was different in New York in those days. Madison Square was entirely residential. The shopping district was from Fourteenth to Twenty-third Street. Of course there were no motor cars, but instead horse-drawn stages rolled up on Fifth Avenue. Horse-drawn streetcars ran on other avenues and crosstown streets."[4]

For Grandmother Hall, education of the children was of great importance. Eleanor had French governesses and German maids, who took her to and from her classes, and she soon spoke French as well as English. Once in a while her father came to visit, but he did not always come when he had promised he would. Then, on August 14, 1894, her father died.

Eleanor refused to believe it. She continued to live with him in her fantasies. But are fantasies lies? The habit of lying stayed with Eleanor, who could easily tell a lie to avoid being punished.

During a trip to France when Eleanor was six years old, she was briefly placed in a convent near Paris to learn French and also to be out of the way because her mother was pregnant with Hall. The other little girls spoke no English, and they stayed away from the somewhat odd American child. Mostly Eleanor wandered by herself around the gardens. One day one of the little girls swallowed a coin and the sisters were very much concerned. The child was the center of attention, and everyone was very kind to her. Eleanor watched. Then she went to one of the sisters and told her that she too had swallowed a coin. She was not a very convincing liar. Her mother was sent for at once, and six-year-old Eleanor was sent away in disgrace.

After Hall's birth, Eleanor returned to America with her mother and two small brothers, but without her father. She was told that he was ill and had to remain in a sanitarium for a while. "We lived in New York that year without my father," Eleanor remembered. "I slept in my mother's room, and remember the thrill of watching her dress to go out in the evenings. She looked so beautiful I was grateful to be allowed to touch her dress or her jewels."[5]

Later, living with Mrs. Hall, Eleanor realized that her grandmother had no sense for beautiful clothes. Women at that time wore layers of petticoats, voluminous floor-length skirts, and high-necked shirtwaists. Beneath all this was a tightly laced corset to give the ladies the shapely hourglass silhouette. The hair was kept long of course, pinned up into a pompadour on top of which a richly embellished hat was pinned. Young girls wore skirts above their knees, even if they were very tall and very thin, as Eleanor was. From the first of November until the first of April, she had to wear flannels from her neck to her ankles, long petticoats and long black stockings—and of course the high-buttoned or high-laced shoes that were supposed to keep the ankles slim.

In the summers, they stayed at Tivoli, the grandmother's country home in the Hudson Valley. The rooms were big with high ceilings and chandeliers for candles, as there was neither gas nor electricity. Cold baths were taken in the mornings. "How I cheated on those cold baths!" Eleanor Roosevelt wrote in her biography. "More hot water went into them than would have been considered beneficial."[6] But the library at Tivoli was filled with books. Eleanor Roosevelt read voraciously, and no one tried to censor her reading.

Aunt Pussie, "a fascinating and lovely creature" to her young niece, taught Eleanor to listen to music and took her to the theater, where she arranged for her to meet the great Eleanor Duse. One day when her grandmother told her to go to a charity bazaar with a friend, "instead of going to the bazaar we went to see a play, 'Tess of d'Urbervilles.' We sat in the peanut gallery and were miserable for fear of seeing someone we knew."[7]

It would appear that Eleanor Roosevelt was not always that paragon of virtue she was made out to be and which some people objected to as bothersome. She had a mind of her own and she used it. Soon she had the opportunity to use that mind to an even greater degree. In 1899, just fifteen years old, Eleanor was sent to Allenswood, Mlle. Souvestre's school in South Fields, England. (Mlle. Souvestre was French, but the siege of Paris during the Franco-Prussian war had been such an ordeal for her that she had moved to England.) She sailed with Mrs. Stanley Mortimer—her Aunt Tissie (sister of Anna Roosevelt)—and her family. "When Aunt Tissie deposited me at the school I felt very lost and very lonely," she wrote.[8]

Only French was permitted to be spoken, just three baths a week were allowed, and the girls had to make their own beds. Bureau drawers and closets were inspected, and any girl whose drawers were out of order might return to her room to find the entire contents dumped on her bed for rearranging.

There were classes in Shakespeare, German, Latin, and music, and Mlle. Souvestre, an elderly, white-haired lady, soon took a special interest in the awkward young American girl. So, "by Christmas I was quite happy and at home in the school," Eleanor wrote in her autobiography. "Christmas Eve and Christmas Day were spent with my Aunt Tissie and her family at the Claridge in London. I had a stocking and many gifts."[9]

Later on, Aunt Tissie lived in Paris, and accompanied by a maid, Eleanor went there quite often. Summer holidays were spent with the Mortimers at St. Moritz in Switzerland. And the following Christmas holidays, Eleanor went with a girlfriend and a chaperon alone to Paris. "I was getting to know Paris and to feel able to find my way about and to decide what I should like to do if ever I were free to plan my own days. She had her first Parisian dress made by a small dressmaker. "I still remember my joy in that long, dark red dress."[10]

The following Easter, Mlle. Souvestre invited Eleanor to accompany her to the south of France and Italy. They stayed with an artist in his villa in Fiesole, dined in cafés overlooking the Mediterranean in Marseilles, ate bouillabaisse and drank *vin rouge*.

The young woman who returned from the Continent to her home in New York no longer was the shy little girl who had left, and she could not adjust. After begging and begging to be permitted to return to Europe, she was told that she could go if she could find someone to chaperon her on the crossing. "I had my first long, tailor-made suit made for me, the skirt trailed on the floor and it was oxford gray," Eleanor wrote. "I was enormously proud of it and engaged a deaconess to take the journey to London with me and return by the next boat. She was sea-sick during the entire trip and I never saw her."[11]

There were more journeys with Mlle. Souvestre: a Christmas in Rome in an old pension, visits to Belgium, Germany, and Austria. "Mlle. Souvestre taught me how to enjoy traveling. She liked to be comfortable, she enjoyed good food, but she always tried to go where you would see the people of the country you were visiting, not your own compatriots. She always ate native dishes and drank native wines."[12]

One morning in Florence, Mlle. Souvestre told Eleanor that she was exhausted, handed her a Baedeker, and told her to explore the city on her own. So, sixteen-year-old Eleanor ventured forth. "Innocence is its own protection," she wrote many years later. "Perhaps Mlle. Souvestre realized that I had not the beauty which appeals to foreign men and that I would be safe from their advances."[13]

She was young, tall and slim, with chestnut hair and blue eyes. It is unlikely that the young Italian men did not pay any attention to her. But so convinced was Eleanor of her own unattractiveness that she probably did not notice them. In any event, "everyone was most helpful. Even when I got lost in the narrow little streets and had to inquire my way I was always treated with the utmost respect and deference."[14]

In 1902, Eleanor was going to be eighteen, the age when young American girls from the "right" families came out. It was unthinkable not to, so Eleanor had to return to America. Because her grandmother now devoted all of her time to an uncle who, like Eleanor's father, was an alcoholic, and the two remained in the country at Tivoli, the girl moved into the West Thirty-seventh Street house with her Aunt Pussie.

Aunt Pussie, Eleanor's exquisite Aunt Pussie, was always in love or had men who were in love with her. She went through one emotional crisis after another. Eleanor stayed up many nights listening to her sobbing. One day Pussie was so annoyed with Eleanor that she told her she probably would never have the beaux that the rest of the Hall women had because she was an ugly duckling.

Now the business of coming out started in earnest. Attired in a blue tulle gown strewn with rosebuds, a wreath of rosebuds around her pompadour, Eleanor Roosevelt was presented to society at a large theater party and supper, with dancing afterward at Sherry's, the most fashionable restaurant in New York. "I should have two partners, one for supper and one for the cotillion," Eleanor Roosevelt remembered in her autobiography. "Any girl who was a success would be asked by many men and accepted the one whom she preferred at the moment. Your popularity was gauged by the number of favors you took home. I was the first girl in my mother's family who was not a belle."[15]

Presented with her to society at that time were her friends Mary Harriman and Isabella Greenway, who later became a congresswoman from Arizona. Eleanor went home as soon as possible, but there were more and more balls and dances she had to go to. Making her ordeal even worse was the presence of her cousin Alice, daughter of Theodore Roosevelt, the new president of the United States. (Theodore Roosevelt had been vice president and had become president in 1901, when Mc-Kinley was assassinated.) "Alice Roosevelt, who was nearest to my age," wrote Eleanor, "was so much more sophisticated and grown-up that I was in great awe of her." The year before, Alice had come out at "the most gala White House ball since the days of Dolley Madison. . . . That first winter, when my sole object in life was society, nearly brought me to a state of nervous collapse."[16]

At that time, her friend Mary Harriman was starting a new project. Mary was the oldest of six children born to railroad magnate and financier E. M. Harriman and Mary Averell Harriman. Polite society frowned upon women who were exceptionally well educated. Fathers often would not even discuss with their daughters the possibility of going to college. Nevertheless, more and more women from upper-class families began to sign up. The first true women's college, Vassar, was founded in 1861; Wellesley followed in 1870 and Smith, in 1875.

Mary Harriman was studying for her Barnard entrance exam when she heard about the work being done by young women her own age at the College Settlement House on Rivington Street on New York's Lower East Side. She rallied her friends together to start a venture she called the Junior League.

"There was no clubhouse," Eleanor Roosevelt remembered, "we were just a group of girls anxious to do something helpful in the city in which we lived. I undertook to teach the children calisthenics and fancy dancing."[17] Eleanor Roosevelt took the elevated railway or the Fourth Avenue streetcar after work to go home. It was usually dark when she crossed the Bowery. The street was dirty; drunks came out of saloons. "The foreign looking people filled me with terror, and I often waited on a corner waiting for a car, watching with a great deal of trepidation, men coming out of saloons or shabby hotels nearby. But the children interested me very much."[18]

By that time, at various dances, Eleanor had occasionally danced with her fifth cousin, Franklin Delano Roosevelt. Franklin was born on January 30, 1882, the son of James Roosevelt and Sara Delano, and was a direct descendant of Claes Martenszan Van Rosenvelt, who arrived in New Amsterdam about 1649 from Holland.

The Delano family lived in a large Victorian mansion in the Hudson Valley, as Sara's father had made a fortune in the China trade. Sara was one of eleven children, and when her father died she inherited over one million dollars. Her husband, James, was about twice her age. His first wife had died in 1876. Sara was entirely smitten by the dashing and worldly gentleman, and they married in 1880. When Franklin was born his father was fifty-four years old.

The boy Franklin could have anything he wanted: a boat, a pony, anything. He was a beautiful little boy whose long blond curls made him look like a girl. He loved his parents, his home, and the Hudson Valley. Often he would travel with his parents to Europe, and at fourteen, as was customary, he was sent to Groton in preparation for Harvard. In 1900, at the age of seventy-two, James Roosevelt died. His son, Franklin, was just eighteen years old. He became the only man in his mother's life.

Traveling to Tivoli one day on the train, Eleanor accidentally met Franklin, who was going to Hyde Park. He came over to her, they chatted, and when they arrived at Hyde Park, Franklin took her to the car in which his mother was waiting. Sara was draped in black, and Eleanor thought her extraordinarily beautiful. Eleanor had never forgotten that this handsome cousin, when he was sixteen years old, had asked her to dance at a party. She had been fourteen, awkward and unhappy, certain that he only wanted to be kind to her.

The year of Eleanor Roosevelt's coming out, Franklin often came down from Harvard to the various debutante parties. Franklin also was a great admirer of President Roosevelt and frequently was invited to Washington, where Eleanor sometimes stayed with her cousin Alice. Franklin was tall and handsome, a blond young man with blue eyes and easy manners who instantly became the life of the party wherever he was.

Much has been written about how strange it was that this extraordinary young man, who was so very popular and could have had his pick of all the gorgeous debutantes, had chosen "an ugly duckling." It was quite true that Eleanor was different from most of the other debutantes, those giggling girls in their pink and blue gowns, waving their fans and dancing cards and ogling the young men from beneath their long lashes. She was a young woman of the world. She had traveled by herself, she had seen other countries, she spoke foreign languages, and she was aware of what was going on in life. "Cousin Eleanor has a very good mind," Franklin was reported to have told his mother.

One day Eleanor told Franklin about her work with the Junior League. Soon he would appear all the way downtown on Rivington Street to see for himself what his cousin was up to. One of the little girls sat there crying because her mother had not shown up to take her home.

Eleanor and Franklin took the child to the dismal tenement in which she lived and climbed up several flights of stairs. It was Franklin's first encounter with a way of life that had been unknown to him until then. He fell into the habit of picking up Eleanor at the settlement house often when he came to town from Harvard, and sometimes they stopped for tea and knishes at the landmark restaurant Schimmels, which is still in existence.

Eleanor, still convinced of her plainness, could not believe that she meant more to the handsome Franklin than just a cousin to whom he wanted to be kind. Certainly she could not express her feelings. "In my generation it was understood that no girl was interested in a man or showed any liking for him until he had made all the advances. You never allowed a man to give you a present except flowers or candy or possibly a book. To receive a piece of jewelry from a man to whom you were not engaged was a sign of being a fast woman, and the idea that you would permit any man to kiss you before you were engaged to him never even crossed my mind."[19]

When Franklin told his mother that he intended to marry Eleanor, Sara Roosevelt was appalled. Her son, the apple of her eye, the little boy whom she had kept in skirts and long blond curls until he was two years old, was going to abandon her? Her, a widow, who had no one else in the entire world, no one to lean on? Not that Sara needed anyone to lean on. When her husband died, she assumed the management of their estate at Hyde Park and handled her own money. She had always been perfectly able to run her own affairs, as she was independently wealthy and widowed at a young age. Eventually of course, her boy, Franklin, would make a suitable marriage, but not so soon! He was just twenty-one years old, and that girl was nineteen. And why Eleanor, a girl who was so different from the way she herself had been at that age? A girl who traveled alone, a girl about whose father there were all sorts of rumors, and a girl who certainly was not a great beauty.

Sara pleaded and begged: They were too young; Franklin had not finished his studies; Eleanor was only a child. Franklin finally agreed to wait for a year and keep their engagement a secret for the time being. Eleanor wrote Franklin that his mother's feelings ought to be considered first, but "I do hope that some day she will learn to love me."[20]

"My mother-in-law had sense enough to realize that both of us were young and undeveloped," wrote Eleanor in her autobiography, "and she decided to try to make her son think this matter over—which, at the time, of course, I resented. As he was well ahead in his studies, she took him with his friend and roommate on a cruise to the West Indies that winter, while I lived in New York. Franklin's feelings did not change, however."[21]

On October 11, 1904, for Eleanor's twentieth birthday, Franklin gave her a ring he had bought at Tiffany's. At the beginning of December their engagement was officially announced, and the wedding took place on March 17, 1905, in New York.

> The bridesmaids were dressed in cream taffeta with three feathers in their hair, and had tulle veils floating down their backs. Franklin had a number of ushers. He had designed a tie pin for them with three little feathers in diamonds. My own dress was heavy stiff satin, with shirred tulle in the neck and the sleeves. My grandmother Hall's rose-point Brussels lace covered the dress, and a veil of the same lace fell from my head over a long train. My mother-in-law had given me a dog collar of pearls which I wore, feeling decked out beyond description. I carried a large bouquet of lilies of the valley.[22]

"Uncle Ted," the newly reelected president of the United States, gave the bride away. He came up from Washington and first reviewed the St. Patrick's Day Parade on Fifth Avenue. Many of the two hundred guests who came to the wedding had difficulties in reaching the house of cousin Susie on Seventy-sixth Street, as no one could enter from Fifth Avenue.

> The police guarded Uncle Ted so carefully that it was difficult for anyone to come in from Madison Avenue. A few guests arrived after the ceremony was over. . . .
>
> After the ceremony we turned around to received congratulations from the various members of our family. In the meantime, Uncle Ted went into the library, where refreshments were served. Those closest to us did take time to wish us well, but the great majority of the guests were more interested in being able to see and listen to the President. The room in which the President was holding forth was filled with people laughing at his stories. I do not remember being particularly surprised by this, and I cannot remember that even Franklin seemed to mind. We simply followed the crowd and listened with the rest.[23]

Later the young couple left under the usual shower of rice.

Eleanor Roosevelt was now Mrs. Franklin Roosevelt. "I had high standards of what a wife and mother should be," she wrote many years later at the age of fifty-three, "and not the faintest notion of what it meant to be either a wife or a mother, and none of my elders enlightened me."[24]

Chapter 2 _____

Marriage

The honeymoon did not take place right away. Because Franklin had to continue his studies at Columbia Law School, the young couple spent only one week by themselves in Hyde Park. Upon their return to New York, they first lived in a hotel apartment in the West Forties. Eleanor was happy that it had a small room for her brother, Hall, to stay in whenever he came for holidays from school at Groton. Eleanor wrote him daily letters, for it was important for her that he knew a sense of "belonging." During those first weeks and months of marriage, she had little else to do but prepare for the big honeymoon trip to Europe.

Eleanor and Franklin went to London, Paris, Venice, Germany, and Switzerland. Both spoke French and some Italian, Franklin loved to roam through old bookstores, they visited friends and relatives. From all accounts the young couple had a wonderful and harmonious time, as attested by the daily letters Eleanor wrote to her mother-in-law. "You are always the sweetest, dearest Mama to your children and I shall look forward to our next long evening together, when I shall want to be kissed all the time."[1] (It is surprising that latter-day chroniclers did not interpret this letter by insinuating that there was more than a mother-daughter relationship between Eleanor and Sara, as they did when they interpreted Eleanor's letter exchange with the journalist Lorena Hickok.)

When Eleanor and Franklin returned to the States in the fall for the opening of Columbia Law School, Eleanor was pregnant. Her mother-in-law had rented for "her children" a house on East Thirty-sixth Street, three blocks from her own. She had furnished it and staffed it with three servants. "For the first year of my married life I was completely taken care of," wrote Eleanor Roosevelt in her autobiography. "My mother-in-law did everything." For Eleanor, who really had not had anyone take care of her before, this could not have been a totally unpleasant experience. "Like many other young women waiting for a first baby, I was sometimes nervous," Eleanor admitted.[2]

On May 3, 1906, a daughter, Anna Eleanor, was born. Nowhere in all of her writings did Eleanor ever express her feelings about the birth. Babies at that time were born at home. There was no anesthesia, and since one did not even talk about sex, it can safely be assumed that no one prepared a young woman for the realities of a birth. Much is being made today of Eleanor Roosevelt telling her daughter Anna that "sex is an ordeal to be borne." The 1920s were very much Victorian times. That sex was an ordeal to be borne by women was the generally believed and accepted assumption. Most daughters the world over were told the same thing by their mothers, if they were courageous enough to bring the matter up at all. Naturally Eleanor, like all young women of her class, knew nothing about handling or feeding a baby, so a trained nurse immediately took over.

Five other children followed at close intervals. On December 23, 1907, the first son was born. James weighed ten pounds, five ounces. On March 18, 1909, the first Franklin, Jr., appeared. He weighed eleven pounds, but in spite of being such a big baby, he was delicate. He died on November 1. Eleanor, who usually blamed herself for every misfortune that befell her, felt that she had failed as a mother. Ten months later, on September 23, 1910, she gave birth to yet another son, Elliott, named after her father. Two more sons were born to Eleanor and Franklin Roosevelt: Franklin D. Roosevelt, Jr., on August 17, 1914, and John, on March 13, 1916.

During the first ten years of her marriage, Eleanor was always having a baby or just getting over having a baby, she wrote, but she certainly had all the help necessary. The children were taken care of by nurses and governesses — and their grandmother. Sara Roosevelt considered them her own children. Whatever their hearts desired, they could get from her. She concentrated her entire life on her grandchildren. She was always there, ready to help.

"My mother-in-law thought that our house was too small," wrote Eleanor in her autobiography, "and that year she bought a plot and built on East 65th Street two houses, Nos. 47 and 49."[3] One was for Sara, the other for her son and his family. The young couple was not enormously wealthy, but both had adequate incomes from trust funds and no financial worries. But, certainly, Sara's help must have raised their living standard.

With her house and her children well taken care of, Eleanor should have been free to pursue her own interests. However, Sara discouraged her from resuming her work at the Rivington settlement house, warning her that she might bring the diseases of the slums home to her own children. Eleanor obeyed. All she wanted now was to please her husband and her mother-in-law, and do her duty to her children. "I did a great deal of embroidery during those years, a great deal of knitting, and an amount of reading which seems incredible to me now. I doubt if there was a novel or a biography or any book that was discussed which I did not read."[4]

After he was graduated from Columbia and admitted to the bar, Franklin worked for a distinguished law firm in New York. Summers were spent with Sara at Hyde Park, Franklin's birthplace, which he worshipped, or often the entire family would journey to Campobello Island in New Brunswick, Canada, where Sara also had a house. Franklin loved to go sailing in the little schooner *Half Moon*. Life could have been calm and pleasant, "but Franklin had a desire for public service, partly encouraged by Uncle Ted's advice to all young men and partly by the glamour of Uncle Ted's example of becoming President of the United States."[5]

In 1909, Franklin D. Roosevelt accepted the Democratic nomination for the state senate for Dutchess County, site of Hyde Park. For thirty-two years, that district had never elected a Democrat. "My father and grandfather were Democrats," said Franklin, "but in 1904, when I cast my first vote for President, I voted for the Republican candidate, Theodore Roosevelt, because I felt that he was a better Democrat than the Democratic candidate."[6]

"My husband's branch of the family and many of the Roosevelts had been Democrats until the Civil War, when they became Abraham Lincoln Republicans," wrote Eleanor. She herself had been raised in a household and milieu where Republicanism and respectability went hand in hand.[7] "I am a Democrat," she declared, "but I was brought up a staunch Republican—and turned Democrat. I believe that the best interests of the country are in the hands of the Democratic party, for I believe they are the most progressive. The Republicans are,—well, they are more conservative, you know, and we can't be too conservative and accomplish things."[8]

Franklin was elected state senator with a majority of about 1,500, and the Roosevelts moved to Albany. There they met a newspaper correspondent who was to play a major role in Franklin Roosevelt's political life, Louis McHenry Howe.

Eleanor did her duty and rarely thought of what she might want to do. She took care of her large household and children and helped her husband in his political life. In 1912, Franklin came out for women's suffrage and Eleanor was amazed. More than that,

> I was shocked, as I had never given the question serious thought, for I took it for granted that men were superior creatures and knew more about politics than women did, and while I realized that if my husband was a suffragist, I probably must be too, I cannot claim to have been a feminist in those early days. Ever since I had been told that I had no right to go into the slums or into hospitals, for fear of bringing diseases home to my children, I had lost a good deal of my crusading spirit where the poor were concerned.[9]

In 1913, Franklin was appointed by President Wilson as assistant secretary of the navy, and the Roosevelts moved to Washington, where Eleanor had to start a new way of life. A large part of her days was devoted to making calls, ten to thirty a day: Mondays the wives of the justices of the Supreme Court, Tuesdays the members of Congress, and so on. Eleanor felt poorly since she was expecting another baby. In the summer of 1914 she went with the children to Campobello, where they now had a house of their own. It was there that the second Franklin, Jr., was born. Franklin came occasionally to Campobello, but mostly his work forced him to stay in Washington.

The shots that rang out in Sarajevo in August 1914, killing the successor to the throne of the Austro-Hungarian Empire, were heard only very dimly at first in Washington. President Wilson was determined that America should not be dragged into the war that was to become World War I. However, ambulances and food were being sent to Europe, and distinguished groups came from foreign nations to look after the interests of their countries in Washington. Social life became busier and more interesting, but more and more it looked as though America would become drawn into war after all. In March of 1916, Eleanor's last son, John Aspinwall, was born. War was declared on April 6, 1917.

"I did little war work that summer beyond the inevitable knitting which every woman undertook," wrote Eleanor Roosevelt.[10] In the summer, she took her children as usual to Campobello, but the navy was cooperating so closely with England and France that Franklin hardly left Washington. Also staying in Washington was Eleanor's enticing young social secretary, Lucy Page Mercer.

During the winter of 1913–14, Eleanor had engaged this attractive and pleasant young woman of twenty-two to help with her social correspondence three mornings a week. Efficient, pretty, and charming, Lucy soon became almost a member of the family. She came from a patrician background, her mother a famous Washington beauty and her father one of the founders of the Chevy Chase Club. Eleanor liked the young woman for her good manners and exquisite taste, and often invited her to her dinner parties.

During the war years, Eleanor became deeply immersed in her work for the Red Cross. She worked out the accounting system for the canteens that were set up, where Red Cross ladies met the troop trains with soup, coffee, and sandwiches for the soldiers. The volunteers worked in tin shacks. Eleanor also distributed the wool for knitters and collected the finished products. In short, she did everything that was asked of her. In May 1918, the Red Cross proposed that Eleanor go to England to organize a Red Cross canteen there. It was a temptation, but in the end she refused because she felt her first obligation was to stay with her children.

In July, Franklin did go to England on naval business. When he returned some time later, he was seriously ill with double pneumonia. Eleanor took care of his mail, and among the letters she opened was one not meant for her eyes.

For a woman who sees herself as plain and who is married to a handsome husband, to discover his infidelities can be devastating. Yet deep within a homely woman there is a glimmer of hope that, if a man as good-looking as her husband has chosen her, she cannot really be as plain as her mother had told her she was.

When Eleanor Roosevelt, then thirty-four years old, discovered that her husband was having an affair with Lucy Mercer, she was shattered. "The bottom dropped out of my own particular world," she confided to a close friend many years later, "and I faced myself, my surroundings, my world, honestly for the first time. I really grew up that year."[11]

Women then who were confronted with their husbands' unfaithfulness had very few options. Divorces were not common. In order to leave one's husband, one would have to have a place to go, a means of supporting oneself. She could become a governess, perhaps a nurse or a maid. If a woman had some money of her own, her husband usually controlled it. Remarkably, Eleanor had always managed her own money, and soon after her discovery, she earned more by teaching and writing.

Most women of the time may have closed their eyes to their husbands' escapades and suffered silently, but this was not the way of Eleanor Roosevelt. Once she knew that Franklin was in love with Lucy Mercer, she offered him his freedom—but she also reminded him that they had five children and Lucy would have to bring them up in case of a divorce.

Franklin reconsidered. He loved his children, and his mother stated flatly that she would disinherit him if he were to blemish the family name with a divorce. Louis Howe told him that a divorce would demolish his political career. Lucy Mercer was a devout Catholic, and her religion did not acknowledge marriage to a divorced man. Eleanor gave him a choice: Lucy or herself, no compromise. Franklin broke off with Lucy.

Eleanor and Franklin reconciled, and in January 1919 they took a trip together to Europe on the U.S.S. George Washington. On February 10, 1920, Lucy, at twenty-nine, married the fifty-six-year-old Winthrop Rutherfurd, a widower with five children and also a close friend of Franklin. Mr. Rutherfurd was a descendant of a distinguished Massachusetts family and the first love of Consuelo Vanderbilt, later Duchess of Marlborough. Mr. Rutherfurd and Lucy Mercer were married for twenty-five years and had one daughter, Barbara. Winthrop Rutherfurd died on March 19, 1944, one year before Franklin. Lucy Mercer Rutherfurd died of cancer on July 31, 1948. [12]

A broken cup can be glued together, as can a broken marriage, but neither will be the same. "I have the memory of an elephant," said Eleanor many years later to a close friend. "I can forgive, but I cannot forget." [13]

In 1920, Franklin Roosevelt was nominated as candidate for vice president to run with James Cox, Democratic nominee for president. The election was won by Warren Harding and Calvin Coolidge, his running mate, and the Roosevelts moved back to New York, where Franklin resumed the practice of law. Eleanor was determined not to have a winter "with nothing but teas and luncheons and dinners to take up my time." She enrolled in a business school, took a course in typing and shorthand, and found an ex-cook to teach her to cook. "I went to her apartment twice a week and cooked an entire meal which I left for her family to criticize." [14] Her training at the business school undoubtedly came in handy in later years when Eleanor began to earn money of her own.

In spite of my mother-in-law's dejection about my earning money, I think she eventually became reconciled to it, realizing that it enabled me to do many things for which my own income was insufficient. I had begun earning money through teaching, writing and radio work. I can remember my pleasure when I first was able to give some substantial help to the Women's Trade Union League in paying off the mortgage on their clubhouse. During the bad days of the depression, I used the first money I earned through commercial radio work to establish two places where girls who were unemployed and searching for work could have lunch and a place to rest.[15]

In the summer of 1921, tragedy struck the Roosevelt family. As usual, they were vacationing at Campobello, swimming, boating, and sailing. Franklin caught a cold and took to his bed with a sore throat, chills, and fever, and he only got worse. Plus there was a strange insensitivity in his legs. The doctors became apprehensive. A well-known infantile paralysis specialist, Dr. Lovett, came up from Newport and examined the patient long and carefully. Franklin Delano Roosevelt, thirty-nine years old, had polio. He was never to walk again.

Sara Roosevelt rushed back from Europe to be near her son and his family. "Franklin's mother was really remarkable about his illness," wrote Eleanor in her autobiography. "It must have been a terrific strain for her, and I am sure that, out of sight, she wept many hours. But with all of us she was very cheerful."[16]

Eleanor turned out to be an excellent nurse, and with another nurse, Miss Rockey, they together took care of Franklin. He was a tall and heavy man to lift, but the two women managed to do whatever was necessary.

Whether or not the physical aspect of the marriage between Eleanor and Franklin came to an end after the Lucy Mercer affair was never clarified. In fact, even Eleanor never once mentioned the matter in her own voluminous writings. Perhaps she felt that it was an entirely private matter which had no bearing on their public lives. But whatever the case might have been, certainly nursing her husband during that debilitating illness must have created a bond far stronger than the one in a so-called "normal" marriage.

Everything in life that is good is also bad, and everything that is bad is also good. If Eleanor Roosevelt had not experienced the jolt of her husband's infidelity, she might have crumbled under the horror of his paralyzing illness.

"People often asked me how I felt about his illness," she remembered.

To tell the truth, I don't think I ever stopped to analyze my feelings. There was so much to do to manage the household and the children and to try to keep things running smoothly that I never had time to think of my own reaction. I simply lived from day to day and got through the best I could. Franklin's illness proved a blessing in disguise, for it gave him strength and courage he had not had before. He had to think out the fundamentals of living and learn the greatest of all lessons – infinite patience and never-ending persistence.[17]

Sara Roosevelt made up her mind that her son was going to be an invalid for the rest of his life and retire to Hyde Park. Eleanor did not agree, nor did Louis Howe. He moved in with the Roosevelts and put his whole heart into working for Franklin's future. The handling of his mail and the newspapers fell entirely into Howe's hands.

Life went on. The children grew up, and at the age of twelve one boy after the other was sent to Groton. The boys hated it, Eleanor did not approve, yet the procedure had to be followed since it was customary for a Roosevelt.

Louis Howe, in order to get Franklin's interest aroused anew in politics, persuaded Eleanor to do some political work herself. She joined the Women's City Club of New York, a civic organization founded in 1916 that worked to make the city a well run and livable city. As vice president of the club in the twenties, she chaired committees, ran errands, brought flowers for luncheons, and kept after people to pay their dues. And frequently, over tea and her favorite huckleberry pudding at the family home on East Sixty-fifth Street, she lent an ear to projects she would later lobby for.

Eleanor also began to work again for the League of Women Voters. She drove cars on Election Day, bringing people to the polls, and learned about politics. "I saw how people took money or its equivalent on election day for their votes and how much of the party machinery was geared to crooked business. On the other hand, I saw hard work and unselfish public service and fine people in unexpected places. I learned that people are seldom all good or all bad and that few human beings are incapable of rising to their heights now and then."[18]

Family life went on. The boys at school had accidents during football season; Franklin underwent treatments. His legs were placed in plaster casts, and the muscles were stretched a little more everyday. It was sheer torture for him, yet he never once was heard to complain.

The house, with Louis Howe and Nurse Rockey living there, as well as all the children when not at school, became more and more crowded. All the bedrooms were taken, and Eleanor found herself without one. So she slept on a bed in one of the little boy's rooms and dressed in her husband's bathroom. "In the daytime I was too busy to need a room."[19]

One day Eleanor met Marion Dickerman, a young schoolteacher who was interested in working conditions for women, an interest Eleanor had shared ever since her work for the Junior League. (At that time she had checked, among other things, the working conditions of women in department stores. Did they have stools to sit on behind the counters when they were not waiting on customers?[20]) Through Miss Dickerman, Eleanor met her friend Nancy Cook. Miss Cook invited her to preside at a luncheon to raise funds for the Women's Division of the Democratic State Committee. It was the beginning of a warm and lasting friendship.

In 1921, the Roosevelt's daughter, Anna, was fifteen. She went to Miss Chapin's School in New York but it was a set and rigid place, and since Anna was treated as an outsider, she was very unhappy there. She also felt neglected because she was relegated to a small room in the attic at home, and made constant scenes. Eleanor, who tried so hard to keep this difficult household rolling with an appearance of normalcy, one day lost control. On an afternoon in the spring,

> I was trying to read to the two youngest boys [and] I suddenly found myself sobbing as I read. I could not think why I was sobbing, nor could I stop. Elliott came in from school, dashed in to look at me and fled. Mr. Howe came in and tried to find out what the matter was, but he gave up as he looked at me. The two little boys went off to bed and I sat on the sofa in the sitting room and sobbed and sobbed. I could not go to dinner in this condition. Finally I found an empty room in my mother-in-law's house, as she had moved to the country. I locked the door and poured cold water on a towel and mopped my face. Eventually I pulled myself together, for it requires an audience, as a rule, to keep on these emotional jags. This is the one and only time I remember in my entire life having gone to pieces in this particular manner. The effect, however, was rather good on Anna, because she began to straighten out, and at last she poured out some of her own troubles.[21]

When Franklin began to feel better and could walk on crutches, the family moved to Hyde Park for the summer. Eleanor realized that the boys now had to learn how to swim, ride, and do other things that were usually taught by a father. "It began to dawn on me that if these two youngest boys were going to have a normal existence without a father to do these things with them, I would have to become a good deal more companionable and more of an all around person than I had been before."22

Franklin learned to walk at first with crutches, later with a cane, leaning on someone's arm. The family tried hard to ignore any handicap he labored under, and since Franklin never complained, the children soon did not even think of him as handicapped. For many years he went for treatment every year to Warm Springs, Georgia, where the other patients seemed worse off than he, arriving on stretchers, in wheelchairs, on crutches. Polio, that dread, crippling disease, had not yet been brought under control by the Salk vaccine.

One day in 1924, Eleanor, Franklin, and her friends Marion Dickerman and Nancy Cook were having a picnic at their favorite spot in Hyde Park, beneath an old shady tree at the bank of a stream called Fall-Kill. It was fall and soon there would no longer be any picnics. The big house, presided over by Sara, was soon to be closed for the winter, and outings would cease until the spring. On the spur of the moment, Franklin offered the three women a few acres of land and suggested they built a cottage of their own. Everyone thought it was a splendid idea. A young architect, Henry Toombs did the design, and Franklin himself undertook the contracting, making certain that the cottage be built of local fieldstone like the early Dutch colonial farmhouses. By the end of 1925, the house, Val-Kill, was ready for its occupants, and its opening was celebrated with a large dinner party, served on a board across two sawhorses with the entire family seated on nail kegs.

While the idea of the cottage was not to remove Eleanor entirely from the vicinity of her mother-in-law in the big house, it did help to ease tensions between the two women. At the Roosevelt mansion, Sara was mistress, and when Eleanor wanted to entertain there, she always had to consult with Sara first. Eventually the entire Roosevelt clan used Val-Kill as an extended home. Franklin and the children swam in the pool there, and guests often stayed there when there was no more room in the big house.

Marion Dickerman was the assistant principal of the Todhunter School for Girls in New York, and later she became principal. It was a private school with classes from elementary through high-school level. When Miss Todhunter decided to return home to England, she sold the school to Marion Dickerman, Nancy Cook, and Eleanor Roosevelt. Franklin liked the idea very much. Eleanor began teaching the higher grades in American history, English, and American literature there in 1927. Later she tried some courses in current events, taking the students to the New York City courts and tenements in many parts of the city.

In 1928, Franklin D. Roosevelt was elected governor of New York. Once again, the Roosevelts moved to Albany, but this time it was into the Governor's Mansion. Eleanor commuted. Since she loved teaching, she continued to go to the Todhunter School three times a week. But she also accepted an invitation to organize the women's end of the New York City office for the national Democratic presidential campaign. The days she taught at the school she came into the office at noon and stayed until her work was finished, often long after midnight. The other days she came in at nine and stayed well into the evening. She concentrated on organizing the office, handling all the mail, greeting visitors. Although Eleanor still hesitated about speaking in public, more and more invitations came her way to give lectures and to write articles. "Women Must Learn to Play the Game as Men Do" was the title of an article she wrote for *Redbook* magazine and was paid $500.00 for.

A man who had a tailor shop in Albany during the years FDR was governor remembered Mrs. Roosevelt coming in carrying armloads of clothes which her children had outgrown. "Mrs. Roosevelt always had them mended and the missing buttons replaced before she gave them away."[23]

My husband, who loved being on the water, found that the state of New York had a small boat used by state officials for canal travel on inspection trips. He decided to use it himself during the summers for the same purpose. Walking was difficult for him and he asked me to go into the institutions to check how they were being run from the point of view of overcrowding, staff, food, and medical care. At first my reports were highly unsatisfactory. I learned to notice whether the beds were too close together, and whether they were folded up and put in closets or behind doors during the day, and I learned to watch the patients' attitudes toward the staff. Before the end of our years in Albany I had become a fairly expert reporter on state institutions.[24]

Franklin D. Roosevelt was reelected governor of New York in 1930. In 1932, he started his campaign for the presidency of the United States. Eleanor remembered, "Franklin did not tell me when he decided to run for the Presidency, but I knew that for a year or more everything that Louis Howe had undertaken for my husband had been with the idea of broadening his acquaintanceships and knowledge of conditions throughout the country."[25]

Instantly, people started to attack him. The Republicans planned to issue a statement claiming that infantile paralysis was a progressive disease which eventually affected the brain.

"A man who chooses to hold public office must learn to accept slander as part of the job and to trust that the majority of people will judge him by his accomplishments in the public service," stated Eleanor Roosevelt.

> I can hardly remember a campaign in which, in our village of Hyde Park, scurrilous things were not said about my husband. They insinuated even that my husband did not have infantile paralysis but some other disease which was progressive and would eventually attack his brain. A man's family also has to accept it. In my husband's case even his little dog, Fala, came in for his share of false accusations. All people in public life are subjected to this type of slander. Circumstantial evidence can almost always be produced to make stories that are circulated about their private lives seem probable to people who want to believe them.[26]

The night before Franklin was nominated, the Roosevelts sat up until morning in Albany in the Governor's Mansion. With them were many friends and political advisers, among whom were Judge Samuel I. Rosenman and his wife, Dorothy. Judge Rosenman had been a counselor to FDR throughout his years as governor.

"Franklin asked my husband to come to Albany to the executive mansion to wait with him for the results of the nomination by the Democratic Convention in Chicago," remembered Dorothy Roseman, who now lives in New York.

> "Bring Dot along also," Franklin told my husband. He liked women who were interested in politics, and I was involved in a project concerning public housing. We spent three days in Albany waiting. At the airport in Albany, ready and waiting was a plane,

poised to take FDR and his immediate family, but also my husband, to Chicago. It was the first time that a public figure, such as a candidate for the next presidency of the United States, was to fly in an airplane. As soon as the nomination was announced, bedlam broke out. The entire press rushed in asking questions and snapping photos, and someone asked me whether I was not afraid to have my husband going up into the air in that small plane.

I was tired and tense from the three days of waiting and, unaccountably, I burst into tears. This was interpreted that indeed I did fear for my husband's life. A secretary went to Mrs. Roosevelt at the other end of the room and told her of my upset.

Eleanor Roosevelt instantly left whatever she was doing, rushed over to me, and took me into a corner. She would talk to her husband, she told me, and would persuade him not to take my husband on the plane with him.

I cried even harder and between sobs attempted to tell her that I knew how important it was for Sam to go with Franklin and that I was not afraid about his flying. But Eleanor said, "No, no. Love is more important than anything else!"

In the end Sam did go, and they all arrived safely in Chicago.[27]

"I was happy for my husband when he was elected President," wrote Eleanor Roosevelt.

I knew that in many ways it would make up for the blow that fate had dealt him when he was stricken with infantile paralysis. I had implicit confidence in his ability to help the country in a crisis. But for myself I was deeply troubled. It meant the end of any personal life of my own. By earning my own money, I had recently enjoyed a certain amount of financial independence and I had been able to do things in which I was personally interested. The turmoil in my heart and mind was rather great.[28]

Chapter 3

The White House

Life did indeed change for Eleanor Roosevelt . . . very quickly. The Roosevelt home in New York on Sixty-fifth Street, instantly filled with Secret Service agents.

March 4, 1933, Inauguration Day, was a rather solemn event. The country under President Herbert Hoover had been under a great depression, economically and emotionally. Eleanor wrote, "When Franklin became President, it was his desire to make life happier for people. He always felt that a President should consider himself an instrument chosen by the people to do their bidding, but that he also, as President, had an obligation to enlighten and lead the people."[1]

The first thing that happened in the country after the inauguration was that the new president declared a bank holiday. "I was concerned," wrote Eleanor, "because we had been staying at the Mayflower Hotel for two or three days and I had no extra cash. I went to my husband and asked him what would happen if we needed some money, and he just smiled."[2]

In the White House, Eleanor Roosevelt lost no time in shocking the chief usher, Ike Hoover, by pushing furniture around and insisting on running the elevator herself without waiting for one of the doormen to run it for her. This was just not done by the president's wife. She also refused absolutely to have a Secret Service agent following her and insisted on driving her own car. The head of the Secret Service was very unhappy about that and finally brought her a revolver. "At least carry this in your car," he said. Mrs. Roosevelt carried it with her religiously and even took some lessons in target shooting. Many years later, she presented that gun to Garrett Entrup, the son of Les and Marge Entrup, the couple who worked for her at Val-Kill. He had done some house-painting for her and refused to accept any payment. "She seemed to be glad to get rid of it," said Garrett. "I never would have used it on a human being, of course," she commented.[3]

Another first for a president's wife were Eleanor Roosevelt's press conferences. They were restricted to newspaperwomen in order to encourage their employment and also because she did not want to encroach on the territory of her husband.[4]

In 1933, while the Roosevelts were beginning to settle down in Washington, troublesome events were taking place across the ocean, but Americans were more concerned about their own enormous problems. That in faraway Germany, someone called Adolf Hitler, a funny-looking former Austrian housepainter, had become chancellor meant very little to the average American citizen. Yet, when the first trickle of refugees began to arrive in the United States, people did not like it. Letters of complaint almost immediately began to arrive on the desk of Washington's new first lady. "Our country, still in the throes of a great depression, is now invaded by foreigners taking jobs away from Americans," they typically said.

A few years later, Eleanor Roosevelt asked Clarence E. Pickett of the American Friends Service Committee to head a Committee for Selected Social Studies to investigate the validity of the accusations. The study was completed, and Mrs. Roosevelt herself wrote the introduction and came to the conclusion that "it seems more and more evident to me that this group of emigrés will be helping us to revise our economic system, and to find new ways of keeping people employed at high level. We are fortunate indeed to have some of the best trained minds of Europe among us now as citizens and we should welcome them and use them to the limit."[5]

It took several years for Americans to realize that the happenings in Germany did concern them after all and that "no man was an island." As such, "the years from 1934 to 1936 seem to me the least anxious of any we spent in the White House," wrote Eleanor Roosevelt. "The reforms instituted were beginning to put the country back on a more even keel."[6]

Since FDR was physically unable to travel around the country to explore conditions, it was his wife whom he sent in his place. Always after her return, they arranged for a quiet meal together so that he could hear a story while it was still fresh in her mind. FDR wanted to know everything: What the life was like of the fishermen in a little village around the Gaspé River in Maine — not only what kinds of fishing and hunting were possible in that area, but also what the people ate, how they lived, what the farms were like, how the houses were built, what type of education was possible. When Eleanor returned from a trip to Maine, he wanted to know about the farms she had visited, the kinds of homes the people had, how the Indians seemed to be getting on and where they came from.[7]

When Eleanor returned from a tour of army hospitals, FDR wanted to know how the food was. "Very good," Eleanor declared. "How did you know?" he inquired. She told him that she had looked at the menus. "But did you also look into the pots?" he asked. After that she never failed to do so, and one can well imagine the terror of chefs when the president's wife appeared, lifting the lids off of steaming pots. FDR also wanted to know the condition of the clothes on the wash lines in poverty-stricken Appalachia, and he wanted to know about the coal miners in West Virginia. No one who lived in those years will ever forget a newspaper cartoon that pictured Mrs. Roosevelt emerging from a mine with a big black smudge on her cheek and the people standing around saying, "What do you know, it's Eleanor!"[8]

In 1933, all the West Virginia coal miners who had been on strike were now living in tents because they had been blacklisted and evicted from company housing. The tents were worn out, people were ill, and there was no medical care. When FDR heard the story, he declared that those families must be out of the tents by Christmas. Eleanor Roosevelt and several other generous individuals collected enough money for new housing. Using the money she received for her radio shows, Mrs. Roosevelt and a friend established a clinic to take care of the children. One of the first people to help Mrs. Roosevelt in this endeavor was Bernard Baruch, who aided in establishing a school there and visited Arthurdale, West Virginia, even without Mrs. Roosevelt, from time to time.

Many of those young people whose lives had been saved by the relief action later showed up in the armies of World War II. "I thought that this was only possible because of the things that had been done to help their parents in the depression period," wrote Eleanor. "Nothing we learn in this world is ever wasted," she added. "I have come to the conclusion that practically nothing we do stands by itself. If it is good it will serve some good purpose in the future. If it is evil, it may haunt us and handicap our efforts in unimagined ways."[9]

When one reads the autobiography of Eleanor Roosevelt, one can hardly turn a page without her referring to her husband. "Franklin realized that teenagers without jobs had to be gainfully employed." "Franklin took great care and great pleasure in establishing the Civilian Conservation Corps camps." "Franklin cared so much about the people of this country." "Franklin started the National Recovery Act, NRA, the Public Works Administration, the Civil Works Administration."

Life in America did improve during the first two or three years of FDR's presidency. He set up program after program to put people back to work again. And Eleanor traveled endlessly. She looked and probed and reported back to her husband. "My husband." Perhaps her autobiography should have been titled *My Husband.*

Helen Gahagan Douglas, wife of the actor Melvin Douglas, was a great admirer of Eleanor Roosevelt. Both husband and wife were much interested in FDR's New Deal and in the work of the National Youth Administration. A friend arranged for the Douglases to be invited to the White House.

"I remember well my first visit to the White House," wrote Mrs. Douglas.

> Mrs. Roosevelt came to greet us with that smile that warmed people. All at once, I felt at home. . . . We met the President that evening at dinner. He was already seated at the table in the family dining room. When Mrs. Roosevelt presented us, the President turned and looked up with his open, dazzling smile. It always seemed to me that Mrs. Roosevelt invited her guests with one thought in mind — to cross-fertilize energies. There would be a mixed gathering. Old friends, neighbors from Hyde Park, like the Henry Morgenthaus, some members of the large Roosevelt family. Very, very often there would be a newcomer Mrs. Roosevelt had spotted, someone who had never been in the White House before. Mrs. Roosevelt guided the conversation. Even the President followed her lead. It was never to herself that she drew attention, but to her husband. One was aware at all times that Eleanor Roosevelt was the wife of Franklin Roosevelt. She addressed him as Franklin and referred to him as Franklin. She was at one and the same time intimate, informal, and natural with him, yet one was aware of her respect, even in her informality, for the office of the presidency and the person of the President. The President and Mrs. Roosevelt would keep the conversation easy, light, bouncy. The President might question Mrs. Roosevelt about something

she had been doing—might even good-naturedly bait her a bit. Mrs. Roosevelt often would draw the President's attention to a newcomer. "Franklin," she would say, "Mr. X. is doing some interesting work. Mr. X, won't you tell Franklin about it?" The President and Mrs. Roosevelt's zest for their own work was contagious. General awareness of the President and Mrs. Roosevelt's receptivity to information brought a stream of voluntary reports from forty-eight states. The President was reached through his wife. Visitors, messages, mail connected millions of people to the capital. Eleanor Roosevelt flung wide open the doors of the White House. . . .

Mrs. Roosevelt came to the West Coast on a lecture tour. The Philharmonic Auditorium was jammed. There wasn't enough standing room. During the question period someone asked: "Mrs. Roosevelt, do you think your husband's being a cripple has affected his mind?" There was absolute silence in that hall. "Yes, my husband's illness has affected him," said Mrs. Roosevelt. "How could it be otherwise? One couldn't suffer as my husband has suffered and fail to be affected. Suffering has made him more sensitive, more responsive to his fellow men."[10]

While Eleanor Roosevelt traveled for her husband, wrote her newspaper articles, did her radio show, and helped thousands of individuals the world over, she never was too busy to keep in touch with her children. Her only daughter, Anna, had married twice. Her first husband was Curtis Dall; they had two children and later divorced. Her second husband was John Boettinger, a young journalist covering the Roosevelts. Mrs. Roosevelt liked John.

On January 20, 1937, Inauguration Day of FDR's second term in office, Eleanor Roosevelt took time out for a letter to her daughter, telling her: "Darling, I must write you a line before going to bed because I've missed you and John so much all day. We drank your health tonight at dinner and I sent you a wire because it seemed as tho' I had to let you know how much you were in my heart." The grandchildren, Buzz and Sisty, accompanied their grandparents to the inauguration. "Darling," reads another letter of September 1937, written from an apartment Mrs. Roosevelt had rented at 20 East Eleventh Street, in New York. "Mrs. Clark [mother of Anne Clark, twenty-one-year-old John Roosevelt's new fiancée] announced the engagement but Johnny was reasonable and said he would not set a date for the wedding, I hope he will get work first."

"Anna, darling," Mrs. Roosevelt wrote about the same time, "Franklin [Jr.] just blew in from Washington and asked if I'd been reading the papers. His engagement was announced to Ethel Du Pont but he says they are not formally engaged."

Not only did Eleanor Roosevelt keep constant and close contact with her children, she also found the time to spend with her grandchildren.

"Shirley Temple is coming Saturday for a swim and picnic," reads yet another letter to Anna on July 3, 1938. "I have written a line to Curtis [Dall] asking whether he wants me to send for them and where."

"The kids were very happy," Grandmère, as they called her reported later. "I read to them today while Sis sewed and Buzz lay on my sofa. Sis asked me 'how are babies born?' so I explained I hope satisfactorily to you, honestly but not in great detail."[11]

In the spring of 1939, the king and the queen of England visited the United States. After their official visit to Washington and later New York, where Mayor La Guardia had been their host, they paid a visit to the Roosevelts at Hyde Park. "Franklin had a tray of cocktails ready in front of him, and his mother sat on the other side of the fireplace looking disapprovingly at the cocktails and telling her son that the King would prefer tea. The King and the Queen arrived. My husband said, 'My mother does not approve of cocktails and thinks you should have a cup of tea.' The King answered, 'Neither does MY mother,' and took a cocktail."[12]

The visit to Hyde Park by the king and queen turned into a memorable occasion. A serving table collapsed and the dishes clattered to the floor. Sara Roosevelt tried to ignore the incident, but her stepdaughter-in-law, from whom she had borrowed some dishes for that dinner, commented loudly that she hoped that none of her own dishes were among the broken ones. More breakage occurred when the butler, carrying a tray with glasses and bowls of ice, fell down two steps into the living room. The next day the king and queen were treated to a picnic, American-style: hot dogs cooked on an outdoor fireplace by the young Robert M. Morgenthau (later district attorney for the County of New York) and smoked turkey, which their majesties had not tasted before.

On August 21, 1939, Germany and the Soviet Union agreed to a non-aggression pact. On September 1, Nazi bombers darkened the sky over Poland, and Great Britain and France declared war on Germany.

"Darling," wrote Eleanor Roosevelt to her daughter, "I feel sick about the war and want so much to do something that looks beyond, toward building a better peace. We can't go on with ever recurring wars in a modern world."[13] But by and large Americans still did not concern themselves too much with the war in Europe.

1940 was an election year. Was President Roosevelt going to run for an unprecedented third term? More and more people insisted that he must, "that the threat of war was just over the horizon and no one else had the prestige and the knowledge to carry on through a crisis."[14] The president finally was persuaded that if he were nominated he could not refuse. During that campaign, some of the people who were against FDR for a third term were seen wearing buttons saying, "We don't want Eleanor either."

In her own opinion, Eleanor Roosevelt felt that "except in extraordinary circumstances," America should stick to its tradition of a two-term presidency. But those were extraordinary circumstances: Hitler had just invaded Denmark and Norway. "The issue before the United States no longer seemed to be aiding the Allies but of America's defense — perhaps even survival."

Franklin D. Roosevelt was nominated by his party for a third term. On Election Day, the Roosevelt family and FDR's political advisers clustered around the radio in Hyde Park. At midnight the traditional parade from the village appeared with red flares and a band playing "The Old Gray Mare."

Was she proud that her husband had won the election? Mrs. Roosevelt was asked by reporters. "This is too serious a time for the President to feel anything but a great sense of responsibility," was her reply.[15]

As President Roosevelt started his third term in office, many Americans still believed that the war raging in Europe was of no concern to the United States.

In September 1941, Eleanor's brother, Hall, died, a victim of the same disease that had afflicted her father: Alcohol had destroyed his liver. Basically, Hall had been the only family Eleanor had had before her marriage. She loved him and felt responsible for him. His death was a great emotional blow for her. That same month, Sara Delano Roosevelt died at the age of eighty-seven. Yet, there was no time to grieve. War for America seemed to be coming inexorably closer.

For New York Mayor Fiorello La Guardia, Eleanor Roosevelt agreed to take charge of the activities that "were not strictly defense activities but allied and necessary for the protection of the civilian population as a whole." And suddenly, on Sunday, December 7, 1941, war was here!

"Pearl Harbor day began quietly," wrote Eleanor Roosevelt in her memoirs. "We were expecting a large party for luncheon and I was disappointed but not surprised when Franklin sent word a short time before that he could not see how he could join us. By the time lunch was over the news had come of the attack on Pearl Harbor."[16]

"The news of the war has just come," Eleanor wrote to her daughter, Anna, who was living out West at that time,

> and I put in a call for you and Johnny as you may want to send the children East. All plans will change from now on. I'm enclosing a check for Buzz & 20 dollars for Johnny. Get them what they want, & 15 dollars for John's razor & I enclose a card. I'm also sending you some sables of Granny's, is your cheap black fur coat worn out as I'd like to give you mine? Do you want a large table-cloth & large napkins of Granny's or of my grandmother's
> Pa told me Churchill was arriving.

"Elliott left last Saturday with his bombing squadron," reported the next letter to Anna. "Franklin Jr. was not present for the birth of his son."[17]

"We knew that the Pearl Harbor attack had set us back a long way," wrote Eleanor in her memoirs. "We had been denied the wherewithal to fortify our islands in the Pacific by people who backed their representatives in Congress in the feeling that Japan did not want war with us. Many believed that only our insistence on preparation for war would force Japan to make war on us."[18]

European dignitaries arrived in Washington. King Peter of Yugoslavia came, and the king of Greece. The Soviet foreign minister, Molotov, brought along a roll of sausage, a chunk of black bread, and a pistol.[19]

Two youngsters, returning with their parents in a car from a summer vacation in the Adirondacks, spied the presidential car speeding toward New York. Franklin D. Roosevelt was deep in conversation with a visitor from Canada, Prime Minister Mackenzie King. The president did not notice the excited small faces and the frantically waving hands, but his wife did. Eleanor waved back to the children and gave them her big, warm smile.

Churchill almost seemed to commute between London and Washington, and Eleanor did not particularly like his ever-present cigar. But in 1942, she herself undertook a journey to wartime England. It was important to the British people that Americans realize what a big role their women were playing in the war. Since it was known that Eleanor Roosevelt wrote a daily newspaper column and also made frequent speeches, the story would go directly to the people.

A red carpet was rolled out at the station when Mrs. Roosevelt arrived in London. Only a very small fire was burning in the enormous sitting room of her suite at Buckingham Palace. A bomb had dropped right through the palace roof, destroying their majesties' rooms. Never very conscious of clothes and aware of the fifty-five-pound baggage limit on the airplane, Eleanor had brought only a sparse wardrobe. A newspaperwoman noted that Mrs. Roosevelt's shoes had holes in their soles. A new pair was sent from Washington. Eleanor had a close look at the devastation wrought by war.

Many of her meals in London were taken at the American Women's Club. Mrs. Martha Mayer, a refugee from Hitler's Germany, worked as a cook there. When she was told that Mrs. Roosevelt was visiting England and that she would have to prepare her meals, she became very excited. She had some American friends living in England, and she consulted them as to Americans' favorite dishes. "Americans are not very particular about food," she was told. "However, they do love corn." And so, Mrs. Mayer cooked everything she could possibly think of that could be made with corn: corn on the cob, corn fritters, corn muffins, creamed corn, buttered corn.

The director of the club, a haughty and stern woman, instructed the staff to disappear as soon as Mrs. Roosevelt arrived. Only waitresses were permitted in the pantry and dining room. On the last day of her visit to England, Mrs. Roosevelt expressed her wish to see the pantry, and Mrs. Mayer wanted to see her so very much. She had come to England with only two skills: to play the piano and to cook. Since she could not earn a living by playing the piano, she became a cook. She had heard so much about America's first lady that it became her biggest wish to see her in person. "I retreated to the far corner of the pantry," she remembered, thinking that she would melt with the wall and that Mrs. Roosevelt would never notice her. Eleanor Roosevelt entered the pantry, took a quick glance around, and marched straight up to Mrs. Mayer.

"Thank you so much for all those wonderful meals you cooked for me," she said as she held out her hand to shake the one of Mrs. Mayer. "The only thing that surprised me though," she said while still holding Mrs. Mayer's hand, "was that the English now seem to like corn so much. Don't they think it is awfully fattening?"[20]

Among the many world-renowned visitors to Hyde Park during those years was Madame Chiang Kai-shek from China. "She was awfully hard to please," remembered one state trooper in Hyde Park during World War II. "Madame Chiang insisted on driving her own car, and when she ran out of gas she was outraged that no gasoline station was open on a Sunday, and besides, we had gasoline rationing."[21]

"The men found Madame Chiang charming, intelligent and fascination," wrote Eleanor Roosevelt about that visitor. "But they were all a little afraid of her. A little, slim figure in Chinese dress, she made a dramatic entrance, but she also could be cruel." At a dinner party at the White House, the labor leader John L. Lewis was also present and had some dispute with FDR. The president turned to Mme Chiang. "What would you do in China with a labor leader like John Lewis?" he asked. Mme Chiang did not say a word. "But her beautiful small hand came up and slid across her throat."[22]

Another visitor to Hyde Park was the Dutch Princess Juliana, who later became queen. "Mrs. Roosevelt brought her right over to me at the booth at the entrance to the Roosevelt estate," remembered the state trooper. " 'This is . . . one of our good men,' she explained to the princess."

> Then she would look at the book in my hand and would ask what I was reading. Fortunately it was not a magazine with girls' pictures. If it was a book she knew, she would discuss it with me. Mrs. Roosevelt was the most considerate person I knew. Often at night, when I was on guard, it was very quiet and dark there in the booth at the entrance to the grounds around the mansion. Sometimes you could not help but doze off. Mrs. Roosevelt often came home late from New York, driving herself and without any Secret Service men. Sometimes it would be one or two o'clock in the morning. And always, just when she was about an eighth of a mile away, she would honk her horn. It was quite clear to me that she did this in order to alert me to her coming and not to embarrass me by finding me asleep. So when I heard her honking the horn, I would quickly pull myself together and then she would arrive and say very friendly: "Good evening, how are you? A very pleasant evening tonight, isn't it?"[23]

The press wrote many stories during the war years about Mrs. Roosevelt's travels—not all of them friendly. "Women should stay home and mind the children," was the sentiment expressed by not a few. That those strenuous journeys were undertaken in the service of her country was not pointed out too often.

"The day I arrived home from England," wrote Mrs. Roosevelt in her memoirs, "we had a large dinner for the President of Ecuador, who was to be an overnight guest. I should have liked to have at least one evening to catch up on my family, for I had been away several weeks, but this is a pleasure a public person cannot always count on."[24]

Besides her own trips were the trips of her husband, about which even his wife knew very little.

But ignoring her critics, Eleanor Roosevelt continued doing what she and her husband thought she ought to do. With only one suitcase, which she mostly packed and carried herself, she traveled to the South Pacific, to the West Coast, to New Zealand, and to Australia. Prime Minister Churchill happened to be in Washington one evening when at dinner in the White House, Eleanor announced that she was going to the southwest Pacific the next day.

"Who is going with you, Mrs. Roosevelt?" he inquired.

"No one," was her reply.[25] After her journey to England she had been criticized so much, she had decided to travel without even a secretary.

The American Red Cross had accepted her offer to look in on various installations and trouble spots during her journeys, and they asked whether she would mind wearing a Red Cross uniform. Mrs. Roosevelt discussed the matter with her husband, and they both agreed that this meant taking less luggage and would also make it easier to visit servicemen and hospitals. Whenever she returned home again, not a few young girls were startled when they answered their telephones to hear a woman saying, "This is Eleanor Roosevelt speaking, and I have a letter [or greetings] for you from your fiancé." Her own four sons were in the service, and traveling with Eleanor wherever she went was the knowledge that the soldier whom she visited in a hospital with an arm or a leg missing could very well be one of her own.

Sometime in 1943, Calvin Johnson, a black American soldier, was eating an ice-cream cone at the counter of the military canteen in Brisbane, Australia. He was just nineteen years old and very downcast. Within the army was considerable racial tension, and even the Red Cross was segregated.

While Mr. Johnson was eating the cone, he heard a commotion at the door and turned around. "What do you know!" he said silently to himself. "It's Mrs. Roosevelt!" Tall and smiling, in her Red Cross uniform with her slip showing just a little, Mrs. Roosevelt went behind the counter and proceeded to shake hands with each and every serviceman. She asked them their names and where they were from. When she arrived before Calvin Johnson, the young soldier shifted his ice-cream cone from his right hand to his left, in order to be able to shake hands with her. Answering her question, he told her that he was from Pittsburgh. At that, her smile grew even warmer and she exclaimed, "We have a Yankee here!" The Australian soldiers laughed and cheered. And then, Mrs. Roosevelt looked Calvin Johnson right in the eyes and asked, "May I have some of that ice cream?"

Calvin Johnson did not know what to do. He thought that if he refused, he would hurt her feelings. But if he were to say "yes," he would do her a grave injustice. This, after all, was a white woman, and she did not really want to eat from his ice-cream cone, he thought. So he just sat there with his mouth hanging open, not knowing what to do. Mrs. Roosevelt, very gently, took the cone from his hand and took a "real big bite from it." Then she handed the cone back to the young soldier. "You see," she said and smiled again, "that didn't hurt at all, did it? You won't ever even miss it."[26]

After Australia, Eleanor Roosevelt went to visit the wounded American solders on Guadalcanal. Admiral Halsey dreaded her coming, and he made no secret of it. After her visit, however, it was apparent that he had changed his mind.

"Here is what she did in twelve hours," he reported later.

> She inspected two Navy hospitals, took a boat to an officer's rest-home and had lunch there, returned and inspected an Army hospital, reviewed the 2nd marine Raider Battalion, made a speech at a service club, attended a reception, and was guest of honor at a dinner. [And, of course, late at night she never failed to type her daily column.]
>
> When Eleanor Roosevelt inspected those hospitals, I don't mean that she shook hands with the chief medical officer, glanced into a sun parlor, and left. I mean that she went into every ward, stopped at every bed, and spoke to every patient: What was his name? How did he feel? Was there anything he needed? Could she take a message home for him?
>
> Wherever Mrs. Roosevelt went she wanted to see things a mother would look for. She went into the kitchens and saw how food was prepared. She chatted with the men like a mother would. Her voice sounded like the one of a mother. Mrs. Roosevelt went through hundreds of wards. As she left, there were many GIs, claiming they had a cold because they suddenly had to blow their noses a lot.[27]

Eleanor Roosevelt herself wrote:

Since this trip was not within easy reach of the enemy, it was
publicized before I left, and countless mothers, wives and sweet-
hearts and sisters wrote to beg me to try to see their menfolk.
When I left home, I took with me a file of cards with the names
and identification numbers of the men I'd been asked to look up.
On my return I had letters to write to hundreds of people, because
during the trip many other boys I met asked me to write their families back home. . . .

I had been to Hawaii, Christmas Island, Penrhyn Island, Bora
Bora, Aitutaki, Tutuila, Samoa, Fiji, New Caledonia; Auckland,
Wellington, and Rotorua in New Zealand; Sydney, Canberra,
Melbourne, Rockhampton, Cairns, Brisbane in Australia; Efate,
Espiritu, Guadalcanal and Wallis. I lost thirty pounds and when I
got home I realized I was more tired than I had ever been in all my
life.[28]

Mrs. Roosevelt wrote upon her return to Washington:

One development gives me great hope for the future. Women have
always come to the fore in wartimes, but I think in WWII, they
took responsibility in more fields than ever before—in factories,
on the farms, in business, and in the military services. They were
an indispensable part of life. This was true in Great Britain, in
Australia, in New Zealand, in France and all the occupied countries in Europe, in Russia and in the U.S. Women have also become conscious of the need to take part in the political life of their
country. In the European countries more women today are playing
an active role in public life than would have been possible before
the war and I am sure we are going to see great developments in
the Asiatic area too. This, to me, is a hopeful sign, for women will
work for peace as they have worked for war.[29]

Other journeys followed. The president insisted that his wife take a
thirteen thousand–mile plane trip in the Caribbean area. The servicemen there felt neglected and unhappy because they could not do what
they thought of as a "more important job." Yet, they had to be there to
watch for submarines, and the president wanted them to know that he
thought they were doing a vital task.

More criticism was heaped on Eleanor Roosevelt by the press each time she undertook an even more strenuous journey on behalf of her country. Since that criticism was equally vicious no matter what she did, this time Mrs. Roosevelt took her secretary, Malvina Thompson, with her. The journey lasted from March 4 to March 28, 1944, and the two women visited Guantánamo, Cuba; Jamaica; Puerto Rico; the Virgin Islands; Antigua; St. Lucia; Trinidad; Paramaribo, Suriname; and Belém and Natal in Brazil.

"Everywhere I went I was treated with the greatest courtesy and consideration," wrote Eleanor, "though some of the top ranking officers were quite frank in telling me they had not anticipated my visit with pleasure. Nevertheless, some of the generals and admirals were kind enough to write to Washington that my trip had been helpful, and I have always hoped that I was able to give the men some pleasure and encouragement, which had been my husband's thought in suggesting this tour."[30]

As the war dragged on, President Roosevelt slowly became a shadow of his former ebullient self. His face was gray and gaunt, his eyes sunken. Another election was coming up in 1944, a fourth term. "I knew without asking that as long as the war was on it was a foregone conclusion that Franklin, if he was well enough, would run again."[31] At the end of that campaign Franklin and Eleanor drove through the streets of New York in an open car during one of the worst rainstorms ever seen in the city. Soon they were drenched to the skin. Sometime before, Eleanor had rented an apartment on Washington Square West, in order for them to have a home in New York.[32] During that campaign trip, they used it for a brief rest.

Thirteen grandchildren, ranging from three to sixteen, attended the inauguration in Washington in January 1944. In February, daughter Anna arrived with her youngest son, Johnny, for an indefinite stay in the White House. Her presence was "the greatest possible help to my husband. She saw and talked to people Franklin was too busy to see and then gave him a digest of the conversations. She also took over the supervision of his food. In fact, she helped him in innumerable ways. Everything she did was done capably and she brought to all her contacts a gaiety and buoyancy that made everybody feel happier because she was around."[33]

In spite of all the care, Franklin's health deteriorated rapidly. Yet, he was determined to go to Yalta for the meeting with Churchill and Stalin he felt was essential for the days of peace that were to follow the end of the war. He was anxious that it should be made impossible for Germany to start another war. He discussed many possibilities, including reducing Germany to a country more dependent on agriculture than in the past, allowing it only such industry as was essential to a self-supporting state, and making sure that the economy of the rest of Europe would not be so dependent again on Germany for its prosperity. FDR emphasized three points that he felt were important psychologically for Germany: First, that Germany should not be allowed aircraft of any kind, not even a glider; second, that nobody should be allowed to wear a uniform; third, that there should be no marching of any kind. The prohibition of uniforms and parades, he thought, would do more than anything else to teach the Germans that they had been defeated.[34]

On March 1, 1945, President Roosevelt addressed Congress – but for the first time sitting down. He really needed a rest, thought Eleanor, so accompanied by two cousins, Laura Delano and Margaret Buckley, FDR departed for Warm Springs, Georgia, as he had so often before.

On April 12, 1945, while Eleanor Roosevelt was at a benefit for a thrift shop at the Sulgrave Club in Washington, she was called to the telephone. After forty years of marriage, her husband, Franklin, had suffered a stroke in Georgia and died. He was sixty-three years old.

President Roosevelt suffered that fatal stroke while sitting for a watercolor portrait painted of him by the famous Russian emigré painter, Mrs. Elizabeth Shoumatov. She was known for painting the famous and wealthy of American society. Mrs. Shoumatov was also a close friend of Lucy Mercer Rutherfurd, who had asked the President for permission that her friend paint his portrait. (After Winthrop Rutherfurd's death the year before, Franklin Roosevelt had occasionally invited Mrs. Rutherfurd to official dinners at the White House.) Among the President's entourage at the time of his death were his two cousins; William D. Hassett, confidential secretary at the White House; Dr. Bruenn; his secretary Grace Tully; Mrs. Shoumatov; and Lucy Mercer Rutherfurd.[35] When Eleanor arrived from Washington, Laura Delano, FDR's cousin, told her of Mrs. Rutherfurd's presence at the time of the stroke.

Later, while sorting her husband's possessions, Eleanor found a little water color of Franklin, also painted by Mrs. Shoumatov. She had it sent to Mrs. Rutherfurd. "She had long wanted to tell her, Mrs. Rutherfurd replied gratefully, that she had seen Franklin and how helpful he had been during her husband's illness and how kind he had been to her husband's boys. She could not get Mrs. Roosevelt's grief out of her mind, Mrs. Roosevelt whom she had always considered to be the most fortunate of women."[36]

Chapter 4 _____

Alone

Like thousands of women everywhere, Eleanor Roosevelt now had to face life without her husband—alone. "I lay in my berth with the window shade open, looking out at the countryside he had loved and watching the faces of the people at stations," she wrote about her journey back from Georgia to Washington. "Somehow one had no chance to think of it as a personal sorrow. It was the sorrow of all those to whom this man who now lay dead, and who happened to be my husband, had been a symbol of strength and fortitude."[1]

At sixty-three, Franklin Delano Roosevelt had been worn out by the burden of his life and work. Paralyzed for twenty-four years, unable to take a single step on his own, having to be carried by his Secret Service men each time he ventured out, he nevertheless led his country and its people whom he called "my friends" out of a devastating depression and rescued the entire world from the menace of Hitler.

But Eleanor Roosevelt was not a woman who permitted herself to dwell on the past. After Franklin was buried in the Rose Garden at Hyde Park, as had been his wish, she returned to Washington to pack up her things in the White House.[2] President Harry S. Truman and his wife, Bess, both urged her to take her time in moving out, but Eleanor was determined to leave at once.

I realized that in the future there would be many important changes in my way of living but I had long since realized that life is made up of a series of adjustments. I had to face the future as countless other women have faced it without their husbands. I had few definite plans but there were certain things I did not want to do. I did not want to run an elaborate household again. I did not want to cease trying to be useful in some way. I did not want to feel old. As time went on, the fact that I kept myself busy and well occupied, made my loneliness less acute. If you have work to do and do it to the best of your ability, you will not have much time to think about yourself.[3]

Eleanor Roosevelt decided to make Val-Kill her permanent home, and in New York she moved into the apartment she had rented in 1942 at 29 Washington Square West.

In her own writings, Eleanor Roosevelt never touched on intimate private matters. The closest she came to discussing her married life with Franklin were the following words in her autobiography.

All human beings have needs and temptations and stresses. Men and women who live together through long years get to know each other's failings; but they also come to know what is worthy of respect and admiration in those they live with, and in themselves. My husband and I had come through the years with an acceptance of each other's faults and foibles, a deep understanding, warm affection, and agreement on essential values. He might have been happier with a wife who was completely uncritical. That I was never able to do, and he had to find it in other people.[4]

As usual, Eleanor Roosevelt was too hard on herself. Had FDR wanted merely an adoring bride who had no mind but her husband's, he would not have fallen in love with the young woman who took him to the slums on the Lower East Side of New York. Without the criticism of his wife, Franklin Delano Roosevelt might have given in to being an invalid on his country estate in Hyde Park. Without Eleanor's criticism, he might not have become one of the greatest presidents of the United States. And perhaps without the guidance and example of Franklin, Eleanor might not have become the "First Lady of the World."

Less than a month after FDR's death, the war in Europe came to an end. On that day, May 8, 1945, a cab was driving down Fifth Avenue. The streets were teeming with revelers. Everyone was shouting, laughing, singing. At Twenty-third Street, a policeman stopped the cab. He told the driver that Mrs. Roosevelt was swamped by a delirious crowd, and he asked him to wait while he brought her over. The driver was overwhelmed. He told her how honored and privileged he felt to have her in his cab, especially on that day. Uncharacteristically, Eleanor Roosevelt did not say much. In the mirror, the driver saw that she did not even smile. He took her to her apartment on Washington Square. "Mrs. Roosevelt," he asked, "aren't you happy that the war is over?" "Oh, of course," she replied, "I am very happy for everyone. However, the war is not over for me. My sons are in the Pacific."

What she did not say was that her husband had given his life to win that war.[5]

In Greenwich Village, Eleanor Roosevelt soon became a familiar sight. She walked Fala, her husband's little black Scotty, in Washington Square Park; she shopped at Wanamaker's on East Eighth Street and chatted with the salesladies; she had tea at small cafés in the narrow, cobblestoned streets, striking up conversations with strangers. She found that the vegetables at Balducci's — which was then just a small grocery store on Greenwich Avenue — were always fresh and well worth the slightly higher price; she would stop for Louis Sherry vanilla ice cream at the counter of Bigelow's, a popular drugstore on Sixth Avenue, before crossing the street to make her usual visit to the Women's House of Detention to see whether she could be of help to the inmates. Prisons! On one morning at the White House, Mrs. Roosevelt had left without saying good morning to her husband because she was to inspect a prison in Baltimore. On his way to his office, the president asked her secretary where "his Missus" was. "She is in prison, Mr. President," the secretary replied. "I am not surprised," said Franklin. "But what for?"[6]

While living in Greenwich Village, Eleanor even took long walks down to East Houston Street to buy potato knishes at Schimmel's, the place where she used to stop for tea so long before after her work at the settlement house, when young Franklin had picked her up.

Eleanor had her hair done in a salon on West Eighth Street. Soon after the owner died of cancer, she was scheduled to give a talk there on behalf of the Cancer Fund. It was raining heavily that day. A large crowd of women were gathered before the shop, which had not yet opened its doors. Two ladies who had come all the way from Westchester were standing amid the angry, complaining crowd. Next to them stood a tall woman who did not say a word. Like everyone else, she was soaking wet. The two ladies glanced at her, then took a closer look, nudged each other, and shook their heads. It couldn't be! But it was. Eleanor Roosevelt, the guest speaker, was waiting too for the doors to open.

What's more, she had been accidentally knocked down by a station wagon on her way to the salon and would be laid up for several weeks with a torn ligament in her ankle.

Eleanor Roosevelt and Greenwich Village went well together. She loved the neighborhood and the neighbors loved her. By the end of 1945, she had gotten used to her new life-style. At sixty-one, she found that she had just as much to do as she had before, if not more. But financial matters were a concern. Since she never consented to accept her widow's pension as the president's wife, she had to cut down and earn enough money to meet her obligations, which she did by writing, appearing on radio and later television, and reading manuscripts for the Junior Literary Guild.

One day while Eleanor was in her Washington Square apartment, she received a phone call that was to change the entire structure of the rest of her life. The call was from President Truman, who told her that the first organizing meeting of the United Nations General Assembly would be held in London in January 1946, almost at once. Would she be willing to serve as a member of the United States delegation?

"That's impossible!" was Mrs. Roosevelt's first reaction. How could she help organize the United Nations when she had no background or experience in international affairs? Yet the president had had enough confidence in her to ask her, and her children, her secretary, everyone urged her to accept. Eleanor herself firmly believed that the United Nations was the one hope for a peaceful world. She accepted.

President Truman's nomination had to be approved by the United States Senate. Some senators protested, especially the one from Mississippi who violently opposed Mrs. Roosevelt's stand on racial discrimination. Nevertheless, her nomination as a United States delegate to the United Nations was confirmed.

In late December 1945, Eleanor embarked on her journey to England. Since no one had informed her that she was permitted to take a secretary, she traveled alone. The *Queen Elizabeth,* which during the war had served as a huge troop transport ship, was still painted gray. On New Year's Eve, Eleanor Roosevelt went to bed in her cabin at 8:30. "Anna darling," reads one of her letters to her daughter. "Just a line from the ship to tell you I am comfortable & tho' the responsibility seems great I'll just do my best. A world of love darling, Mother."[7]

The U.S. delegation consisted of several distinguished members. Among them were former chief foreign affairs adviser, John Foster Dulles — not an admirer of Eleanor Roosevelt — and Republican Senator

Arthur H. Vandenberg, before the war a great champion of isolationism. During the journey, Senator Vandenberg asked Mrs. Roosevelt whether she would serve on Committee Three. She would serve wherever she was needed, she replied, but she would like to get as much information as possible on Committee Three, whatever that might be.[8]

As Eleanor Roosevelt learned more about her work, she soon realized why the distinguished gentlemen had recruited her for that particular committee. Committee Three dealt with humanitarian, educational, and cultural questions, and Mrs. Roosevelt gathered that the consensus of the other delegates was that she could not do much harm there.

The first business of the assembly was the election of the first president of the UN. The choice was Paul-Henri Spaak of Belgium, a man whom Eleanor Roosevelt called "a wonderful diplomat, an eloquent orator and a statesman of stature." It so happened that soon after the arrival of the American delegation, Spaak was to celebrate his birthday. A young Belgian staff member approached an American liaison official, Alger Hiss, and told him that a surprise birthday party was planned for Spaak by his wife. The Belgian staff member had asked Mme Spaak what she thought her husband would like as a birthday present. After long consideration, she said that she could not really think of a single thing that her husband would need or want—except Mrs. Roosevelt as a guest at the party.

Hiss relayed this conversation to Mrs. Roosevelt, who "responded with almost girlish delight. She actually seemed to be flattered."[9] But by and large, Eleanor Roosevelt was fully aware that, as the only woman in her delegation, she was not very welcome. So, her first plan of action was to become friendly with the women in the other delegations—there were only about sixteen—and she invited them all for tea in her hotel sitting room. Even the Russian women came, bringing an interpreter.

"I found that often a few people of different nationalities, meeting on a semi-social basis, could talk together about common problems with better results than when they were meeting officially."[10]

While Mrs. Roosevelt was working on Committee Three, a subject came up that was of deep interest to her. Thousands of displaced war refugees had been in Germany when the armistice was signed: Ukrainians, Belorussians, Poles, Czechoslovakians, Latvians, Lithuanians, Estonians, and many others. Since they did not want to return to live under communism in their own countries, they were herded together in temporary displaced persons camps. The position of the Soviet Union was that any war refugee who did not wish to return to his country of origin was either a quisling or a traitor. They insisted that the refugees in Germany should be made to return home by force if necessary and accept whatever punishment might be meted out to them. But the position of the Western countries, including the United States, was that a large number of those refugees were neither traitors nor quislings and that they must be guaranteed the right to choose whether or not they would return to their homelands.

Eleanor Roosevelt decided that she wanted to see the situation in the camps with her own eyes, so a visit to Germany was arranged for her. It was 1946, and many of the great cities she remembered from her travels — Frankfurt, Cologne, Munich, Berlin — were no more than piles of rubble.

"One day an American lady appeared in our camp," remembered a Mrs. Anastasia Holubowich, who had come from Vitebsk, Belorussia. During the war, their city was captured by the Germans, and she, her husband who was a farmer, and their two teenage children were taken by the Nazis to Germany by cattle cars to serve as slave laborers to the "Master Race." Along with produce, calves, and pigs, they were allocated to a German farm family. When the war ended, they were freed.

Along with thousands of ragged, haunted, and emaciated victims of the Third Reich, they appealed to the United States commanding officer for permission to stay. They were given temporary asylum in a camp in Haar, a little town near Munich. There Mrs. Holubowich gave birth to a third child, whom she named Alexandra. At the time when Eleanor Roosevelt visited the camp, Alexandra was six months old, and since the American lady wished to see all the children in the camp, Alexandra's mother presented her baby in her arms. Mrs. Holubowich now lives in Florida, and she remembers still how nicely dressed the visitor was and what a kind smile she had.[11]

When Eleanor Roosevelt returned home to go on with her work, President Truman asked her to become a delegate to the General Assembly on the Human Rights Commission. The commission worked first at Hunter College in New York, carried on in Geneva, then for the following two years moved to Lake Success on Long Island.

"After I had been elected chairman of the Human Rights Commission, we decided that our main task was to write an International Bill of Rights," wrote Eleanor Roosevelt in her memoirs. "We spent most of our time trying to write the Universal Declaration of Human Rights and the Covenants."[12]

The last session of the General Assembly Mrs. Roosevelt attended met in Paris from the fall of 1951 to February 1952. The declaration included the question of whether the refugees in the still existing displaced persons camps in Germany should be considered political deserters or refugees. Meanwhile, in the camp near Munich where Eleanor had asked to see the children, the six-month-old baby Alexandra was now five years old. At about that time, a terrible storm destroyed the entire camp, and the displaced people were transported to another. In that camp, however, everyone was scheduled to be returned to their land of origin.

Terrible scenes took place. Many of the refugees committed suicide by slitting their throats rather than return; people killed each other to escape a fate they considered worse than death; but most were loaded on trucks by force. Mrs. Holubowich, her husband, and three children were also forced onto a truck, but on the road toward the Russian border it had a flat tire. It took many hours to be repaired and, as a result, the truck arrived as the very last at the Russian border.

Back in Paris at a stormy session of the United Nations, a vote was taken on the Declaration of Human Rights. Eleanor Roosevelt had many adversaries, mainly of course the Soviet Union. When she spoke to battle the famous Russian Vishinsky, the delegates from South America rose to leave. "The hour was late," wrote Mrs. Roosevelt, "and we knew that the Russians would delay a vote as long as possible on the theory that some of our allies would get tired and leave. I knew we must hold our South American colleagues until the vote was taken because their vote might be decisive. So I talked about Simón Bolívar and his stand for freedom of the people of Latin America. The South American representatives stayed with us to the end."[13]

At the Russian border meanwhile, where at three o'clock in the morning the soldiers began to unload their human cargo from the last truck, officials stopped them. Eleanor Roosevelt's battle for the rights of man had succeeded. The forced repatriation of Eastern Europeans was halted.

Toward the end of the session in Paris, John Foster Dulles and Senator Vandenberg, the two Republican members of the American delegation, came up to Mrs. Roosevelt and congratulated her. "As you may or may not know, Mrs. Roosevelt, we were very much opposed to your appointment. We thought that President Truman had made a mistake. We take it all back. This was a first rate performance."[14]

James Frederick Green, director of the Commission to Study the Organization of Peace, served with Eleanor Roosevelt on the UN Commission on Human Rights from 1946 to 1953. He recalled:

> Going around Paris with Mrs. Roosevelt was like walking around with the Statue of Liberty. The French just had this tremendous reverence for the Roosevelts, and as she would get out of a car or taxi, the men would all tip their hats and the women would curtsey to her. I think that Mrs. Roosevelt, because she liked the French and spoke French very well, was rather pleased and honored. I also gave a small cocktail party in Paris while my wife was there and we invited Mrs. Roosevelt to the small apartment we had rented. Afterward, the concierge scolded me for not telling him that I was expecting Mrs. Roosevelt. He would have cleaned the steps, he would have cleaned the elevator, and had everything proper for her.
>
> But Mrs. Roosevelt was not the woolly-minded idealist that she was accused of being, not at all. She very much had her feet on the ground. She had total recall for dates and faces and facts and never missed a single meeting. Once during a UN meeting, a Soviet delegate gave a long speech on the horrors of agriculture in the U.S., about the downtrodden farmers and so on. Then he read a description of what conditions were like in Oklahoma. When the session was over, Mrs. Roosevelt asked someone to go to the public library and obtain a copy of John Steinbeck's *Grapes of Wrath.* When the afternoon meeting began, she raised her hand and said: "I was fascinated by the long discussion and description of agricultural conditions in the U.S. But I would like to point out that the final portion of the remarks of the distinguished delegate from the Soviet Union are somewhat out of date, because he was reading from Steinbeck's *Grapes of Wrath,* and it just happens that that was written in the early 1930s, in the depth of the Depression."[15]

In 1952, General Dwight D. Eisenhower, a Republican, was elected president of the United States. When there is a change of administration, every ambassador abroad and to the UN writes a letter of resignation to the incoming president. Eisenhower and the new secretary of state, John Foster Dulles, wanted Mary Oswald Lord to take Mrs. Roosevelt's place in the United Nations.

Many invitations had been extended to Eleanor which she had been unable to accept because of her heavy schedule at the United Nations. Now that she was free, she decided to go home from Paris the long way — around the world.

The first invitation she accepted was from Prime Minister Jawaharlal Nehru of India. As part of the committee to welcome Mrs. Roosevelt to Bombay was an American women's organization. Among this group was a woman who had seen Mrs. Roosevelt many years before when she had been a student at Skidmore College. The visiting first lady, she remembered,

> was wearing a horrible brown velvet dress with a big white bib around her neck and an atrocious hat. The girls had giggled and imitated Eleanor Roosevelt's high-pitched voice. Now, many years later in India, Mrs. Roosevelt's taste in clothes had not improved. She wore a nondescript jersey dress and white sensible shoes. Her hair was not properly coiffured and her face was perspiring. But when she approached the Indian delegation which welcomed her, Mrs. Roosevelt was very careful not to reach out for a handshake and instead, just touched her fingertips to her brow. "What a beautiful woman she is," said a handsome young Indian official to the former Skidmore student. "I have never seen such magnificent blue eyes in such a lovely feminine face. She is the personification of a beautiful soul. You Americans must be very proud of her."[16]

When Mrs. Roosevelt returned to New York, she had to face a personal loss once again. Malvina Thompson, her secretary and friend for thirty years, died after a lingering sickness. "No one can ever take the place of such a person," wrote Eleanor Roosevelt, "nor does one cease missing her."[17] She also had to look for a new job.

"My interest in the United Nations had grown steadily during the six years I served as a Delegate, and later I volunteered to work with the American Association for the United Nations so that I would not be out of touch with the work of the one organization that has the machinery to bring together all nations in an effort to maintain world peace."[18]

Work for the American Association for the United Nations began in the spring of 1953. Since Eleanor had to be at the office on East Forty-sixth Street by nine in the morning, the apartment on Washington Square which had given her a refuge for the first years of her life alone now was too far out of the way. She moved uptown.

Meeting Eleanor Roosevelt in 1953 was Nancy Dubner, a sophomore from Central Connecticut State University in New Britain. Every June, the collegiate councils for the UN student group held a national meeting in New York. Both United Nations and federal government officials gave talks to what was considered the "cream of U.S. students." Nancy studied American history and was very active with the UN group.

"Mrs. Roosevelt did not give a speech to us like the others," remembered Nancy. "With her we would all sit down on the floor, and she would chat with us. She usually spent considerable time with us young people, asked many questions, and really listened to what we had to say. She made us understand that the world's problems and the big happenings in politics influence all our individual lives. At one point, Mrs. Roosevelt invited the board of the student group to come to Val-Kill for a picnic."[19]

Nancy was national vice president, but she could not afford to go to Hyde Park. She thought about that missed opportunity for many years and finally, long after the death of Eleanor Roosevelt, she did undertake the trip, which triggered an important event. But that comes later in the story.

Another woman who remembers Eleanor Roosevelt from the days she served at the American Association for the United Nations is Roma Stibravy. Roma is at present with the United Industrial Development organization. When she was eighteen years old, she was for a while hostess for the American Association. The guest speaker one day was Mrs. Roosevelt, and Roma was to greet her. As was customary, she waited at the top of the staircase, holding a box containing an orchid corsage which she was to present to Eleanor. Mrs. Roosevelt appeared, accompanied by her secretary, and began to ascend the staircase. Pinned to her shoulder was an orchid. Roma, mortified, tried to hide the orchid behind her back, then realized that she would have to shake hands.

"I wished the floor would open up beneath me," Roma still recalls vividly. "But as Mrs. Roosevelt came closer, she smiled at me, calmly took off her own corsage, and pinned it onto the shoulder of her companion. Then chuckling a little, she accepted the corsage from my own unsteady hand."[20]

During the years with the association, Eleanor Roosevelt continued her extensive traveling. An invitation was extended to visit Japan as part of a group of exchange people under the auspices of Columbia University, which acted as host for the Japanese who came to America. The reason why the Japanese specifically invited Mrs. Roosevelt was that the women there were just beginning to function in a democracy. Among the cities she visited was Hiroshima.

"To arrive in Hiroshima is an emotional experience," she wrote.

Here is where the first bomb ever to be dropped on human beings was actually used. The people of the United States believe that our leaders thought long and carefully before they used this dread weapon. We know that they thought first of the welfare of our own people, that they believed that the bomb might end the war quickly with less loss of life everywhere than if it had not been dropped. To see the devastation, the home where orphans were being cared for was to wish with one's whole heart that men could learn from this that we know too well how to destroy and must learn instead how to prevent such destructions. Contemplating the fate of Hiroshima, one can only say: "God grant men greater wisdom in the future."[21]

The journey to Japan was followed by many others. Especially notable were the one to Yugoslavia, where she interviewed Marshal Tito; many to Israel, a country for which she had great love and admiration; and two to Russia. She wrote extensively about the latter in her autobiography:

The most important things I learned about the Soviet Union — and the things that may be most difficult for democratic peoples everywhere to comprehend — came to focus when I visited the medical school in Leningrad. At the institute I asked to see their method in handling children. Thirty-two children taken at birth from lying-in hospitals whose parents had died or abandoned them, were being trained. . . . It was here that the Dr. Pavlov theories were being put into practice. . . . I think I should die if I had to live in Soviet Russia. When I went to Moscow, the Stalinist dictatorship had been replaced by the less fearful dictatorship of Nikita S. Khruschchev. [Khruschchev and his wife later visited Mrs. Roosevelt at Val-Kill.] But the people still existed under a system of surveillance that must cause anxiety and the power over them still seemed to me a hand of steel.[22]

Back in the United States a new challenge arose for Eleanor Roosevelt when a man she greatly admired was running again for the Democratic nomination for president. She firmly believed that Adlai Stevenson, governor of Illinois, would probably make one of the best presidents that America ever had. In 1956, Eleanor Roosevelt was not greatly impressed with the progress of what President Eisenhower called "Modern Republicanism," and so she went "all the way for Adlai."

Mrs. Roosevelt arrived in Chicago for the Democratic convention wearing a blue dress with flowers on it. Later that evening at a strategy meeting at a hotel, she appeared in that same dress. She wore it the next morning for a television appearance and again that afternoon for the opening session of the convention. Soon it became clear that wherever Mrs. Roosevelt went, so went the blue, flowered dress. The reporters began to speculate. Was this an especially favorite, good-luck dress? One of them was bold enough to approach her with the question. Eleanor looked at him with great astonishment and then laughed. "I have been so busy," she explained, "that I did not notice. I brought other dresses of course. Frankly, I had not realized that I wore only this one."[23]

The dress was not a good-luck dress. Though Adlai Stevenson was nominated for the second time that year, he never became president.

More journeys were in the busy schedule of Eleanor Roosevelt: Bali, Morocco, the Far East. Most of them were in connection with official business, and often she was accompanied by one of her grandchildren and her personal physician. At home there were thousands and thousands of lectures, books to write, and letters to answer. "We answered every single letter that came to us," said Maureen Corr, Mrs. Roosevelt's secretary for the last twelve years of her life. "We worked day and night."[24]

The letters came from people all over the country. Mostly they appealed for some sort of help, such as with a political assignment. "I can't do much there and mostly tell them to go to Mr. Eisenhower instead," Mrs. Roosevelt once said laughingly. Sometimes they asked for money. "That I could not give them either because I did not have much myself."[25]

Up to almost the last days of her life, Eleanor Roosevelt continued to earn her own living. One day a request came for her to do a margarine commercial. She knew that she would be bitterly criticized for doing a commercial, but on the other hand she wanted very much to have her voice heard on TV. She did the commercial, but she took the opportunity to remind her audience that there were hungry people in the world.

"It is startling to realize that one is so deeply, fanatically disliked by a number of people," Eleanor Roosevelt wrote in her autobiography. "And yet, while I weigh as honestly as I can their grounds for disapproval, when I felt that I am right in what I do, it seems to me that I cannot afford, as a self-respecting individual, to refuse to do a thing merely because it will make me disliked or bring a storm of criticism over my head."[26]

With all of Eleanor Roosevelt's work — her writing, traveling, lecturing, and work at the UN — she always made time to keep in constant touch with her daughter, four sons, their spouses, and her grandchildren and great-grandchildren. The person to turn to when there was trouble of any sort — financial, emotional, or an illness — was always "Mummy darling," as Anna wrote her.

"Sis darling," wrote Mrs. Roosevelt in February 1957.

> I guess I was more tired than I knew & that was probably why I was so hard hit by whatever bug I had on my last trip. I had pneumonia and near pleurisy but I am back and more rested than I have been in a long time. Sunday I leave on a paid lecture trip and have to write two articles by March 1st. I won't hurry with my $350.00, but will send it later in the spring. Just the next few months expenses are high as I bought a new station wagon and must turn in my car. Of course if you are getting John's insurance policy money [Anna's second husband had committed suicide] and you really feel it will cover all expenses I won't pay but you let me know and I might be able to give you a bit more.[27]

Eleanor Roosevelt's seventieth birthday was celebrated at the Waldorf-Astoria Hotel in New York. Dr. Ernst Papanek, a Viennese educator who was the director of the Wiltwick School for boys, which was especially close to Eleanor's heart, visited her with some of the students. (Famous alumni of that school include Claude Brown and Floyd Patterson.) The boys serenaded Mrs. Roosevelt and brought her one hundred pot holders they had made themselves. Later, at dinner, she announced the gift and invited anyone who wanted a pot holder to step forward. But when a few people actually took her up on the offer, she laughed and shook her head. She had changed her mind, she said, because the boys, after all, had made the pot holders for her.

Every year, the Wiltwick boys were invited for a picnic at Val-Kill. They got hot dogs on rolls which Mrs. Roosevelt personally buttered for them, corn on the cob, and ice cream. After they had eaten, she read them stories: Kipling's "Rikki-Tikki-Tavi" or "The Butterfly That Stamped" or "How the Elephant Got His Trunk."[28]

"I thought for once Mrs. Roosevelt had made a mistake," wrote Dr. Margaret Mead, who was present at one of the picnics for the Wiltwick boys. "Those boys seemed too old for those stories. But they were not restless and they listened raptly. I later found out that they were much younger than their faces looked and realized this was because of terrible deprivations they had suffered until they came to Wiltwick."[29]

Perhaps one of the most poignant stories about Wiltwick is the one of a boy who came to Mrs. Roosevelt after a picnic and asked her whether she remembered him. She replied that indeed she did, and hadn't he been there the year before? "Do you remember my name?" the boy asked then. Mrs. Roosevelt shook her head and apologized. She said that she was getting old and that she often did not even remember the names of her best friends. The boy told her that his name was John Owen, then he ran away. A few moments later he came back and asked again whether she knew his name. "Of course," was her reply. "You are John Owen." He nodded and left. Half an hour later he returned again. "You still know my name?" he inquired. "John Owen!" Mrs. Roosevelt said promptly. "Okay," he said and grinned. "I guess from now on you will know who I am."

The incident impressed Mrs. Roosevelt greatly and she often wrote about it and told it to friends. "There is a desperate need for identification and recognition as an individual all through life to people who, because of circumstances or some limitations in themselves, have not learned to feel they have developed as individuals or have been so accepted," she wrote in her book *You Learn by Living.*[30]

By 1960, Eleanor Roosevelt began to look tired. "You must slow down," people began to tell her, "you really must slow down."

How is a woman such as Eleanor Roosevelt to slow down. There was so much to do, so much trouble in the world, so many people who needed help. A new election was coming up. The question was whether her favorite, Governor Adlai Stevenson, was going to be nominated again, or would Senator John F. Kennedy of Massachusetts. Eleanor declared she could not support Kennedy. The reason she gave was that she could neither forgive nor forget his failure to take a position at the time of the controversy over Senator Joseph McCarthy and his despicable methods of investigation. She was quite firm about this and told it to Kennedy in person.

But there might have been another reason. Eleanor may still have re-membered a day when Joseph Kennedy, father of John and returning ambassador to England, paid a visit to President Roosevelt in Hyde Park. In a book review, distinguished writer Gore Vidal related the fol-lowing story, which he evidently remembered vividly:

"When Mr. Joe Kennedy came back from London during the war," Eleanor Roosevelt began during a luncheon at which Mr. Vidal was one of three guests,

> he gave that unfortunate interview in Boston in which he was . . . well, somewhat critical of us. Well, MY Franklin said, "We better have him down here at Hyde Park and see what he has to say." So Mr. Kennedy arrived at Rhinecliff on the train and I met him and took him straight to Franklin. Well, ten minutes later one of the aides came and said, "The President wants to see you right away." This was unheard of. So I RUSHED into the office and there was Franklin, white as a sheet. He asked Mr. Kennedy to step outside and then he said, and his voice was SHAKING, "I NEVER want to see that man again as long as I live. Get him out of here." I said, "But, dear, you have invited him for the week-end, and we've got guests for lunch and the train does not leave until two," and Frank-lin said, "Then you drive him around Hyde Park and put him on that train," and I did and it was the most dreadful four hours of my life!" She laughed. Then, seriously: "I wonder if the true story of Joe Kennedy will ever be known."[31]

Yet, once John F. Kennedy was nominated for the presidency, she did have him visit her at Val-Kill. Taking him into the kitchen—a room where his head almost seemed to touch the ceiling—she introduced him to her friends, the couple who worked for her. Eleanor found Kennedy to be "a brilliant man with a quick mind, anxious to learn, hospitable to new ideas, hardheaded in his approach."[32] In spite of her protestations never again to campaign actively, she did take part in his campaign for president.

The day on which that visit took place was perhaps one of the hardest in Eleanor Roosevelt's life. The day before, her granddaughter Sally, the teenage daughter of John Roosevelt, had fallen from a horse and died. John Kennedy had offered to cancel his visit, but Eleanor would not hear of it. She never went back on an obligation.

In 1962, Eleanor was still traveling. Letters came to Anna from St.

Moritz, from Campobello, from Israel. This last year of her life she also wrote checks: to godchildren whose school tuition she had taken on, to organizations she always supported. And, like FDR, she prepared a memorandum on how she wanted to be buried: in a plain wooden coffin, covered with pine branches from the woods around Val-Kill.

One would have wished that a woman such as Eleanor Roosevelt would have had an easy time dying, but this was not to be. She was diagnosed as having a rare bone-marrow form of tuberculosis.

Weaker and weaker, Eleanor Roosevelt made her last public appearance on a truck in Greenwich Village, just one block away from her former residence. She was campaigning for Ed Koch (later mayor of New York), who was running for assemblyman. Seventy-eight years old and terminally ill, Mrs. Roosevelt climbed up the ladder and began to speak. As soon as people noticed her, a great crowd gathered. A yellow cab came along, and the driver impatiently honked his horn. Several people hushed him. "Don't you tell me to shut up," the cabbie shouted. "I have a fare here in my cab and he's in a hurry!"

Someone told him that the person speaking was Mrs. Roosevelt. "Eleanor Roosevelt?" He got out of his cab and, letting his fare sit there, listened attentively until Eleanor was finished with her speech.[33]

On November 7, 1962, Eleanor Roosevelt's heart finally gave out — the heart that had encompassed so very many people. Contrary to general belief that a person who loves many, does not love one, Eleanor Roosevelt had a great many close bonds. Her various secretaries became warm and trusted friends; a bodyguard to Franklin and Eleanor, the handsome Earl Miller, and his various girlfriends and wives, was included in the Roosevelt family like an adopted son. A young man she met while first lady, Joseph Lash, who later wrote exhaustive and prize-winning biographies of her, turned into a lifelong trusted friend. Eleanor probably spent more time with him and his wife, Trude, than with anyone else, with the exception perhaps of her personal physician, David Gurewitsch, and his wife, both of whom traveled with her often. Maureen Corr, her secretary for the last twelve years, had a very special place in Mrs. Roosevelt's heart, as evidenced from her own writings.

"There is, I believe, a legend in the Talmud which tells us that in any period of history the heavens themselves are held up in place by the virtue, love, and shining integrity of twelve just men," Adlai Stevenson said in his tribute to Eleanor Roosevelt at the Democratic National Convention in March 1963.

They are completely unaware of this function. They go about their daily work, their humble chores—doctors, teachers, workers, farmers (never lawyers alas, so I understand), just ordinary devoted citizens and meanwhile the rooftree of creation is supported by them alone. Can we doubt that Eleanor Roosevelt's standards and her integrity steadied our own? Long before the civil rights issue moved to the forefront of the nation's consciousness, she was there, earning public abuse for her quiet reminders of the inequalities practiced in our land, she would bid to add to the civil liberties we guarantee, the extra dimension of opportunity without which even rights seem so much emptiness.[34]

It might be added here that long before the women's rights issue moved to the foreground, Eleanor Roosevelt stood up for the things in which she believed, never permitting anyone to deter her because she was "just a woman."

Modern literature, which likes to focus on the salacious and sensational, tries its best to make the story of Eleanor Roosevelt titillating. What about that love affair of FDR's? Wasn't there anything more to Eleanor Roosevelt's relationship with the handsome guard? What about those intimate letters she wrote to her one-time secretary?

Do we really care?

Eleanor Roosevelt gave all that she had. To us. We are living her heritage.

Anna Eleanor Roosevelt, 1887, Huntington, Long Island, N.Y.
''She is such a funny child, so old-fashioned that we always call
her 'Granny.' '' Photo courtesy of the FDR Library.

Eleanor Roosevelt, 1911. Photo courtesy of the FDR
Library.

Miss Roosevelt becomes Mrs. Roosevelt. Eleanor and Franklin on their honeymoon in Strathpeffer, Scotland, August 31, 1905. Photo courtesy of the FDR Library.

"A home of my own." Val-Kill Cottage, 1938. Photo courtesy of the FDR Library.

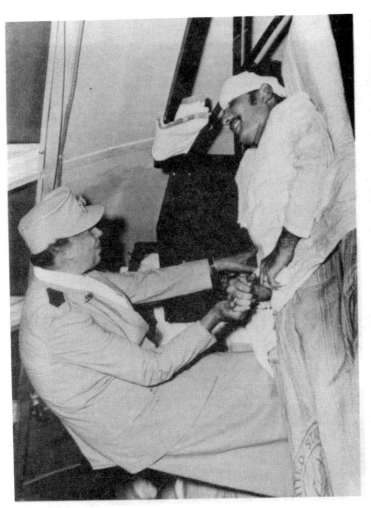

Eleanor in a Red Cross uniform visiting wounded American soldiers somewhere in the Pacific, 1943. She traveled 25,000 miles in five weeks. Photo courtesy of the FDR Library.

President and Mrs. Roosevelt at the 3rd Inaugural, January 20, 1941. Photo courtesy of the FDR Library.

"My most important task." Eleanor with the Declaration of Human Rights, November 1947. Photo courtesy of the FDR Library.

A picnic at Val-Kill for the boys of the Wiltwick School, June 1954. Photo by Olga J. Norbin; used with permission of the photographer.

Eleanor sewing the first ILG label, February 14, 1961. Photo from the collection of Stella K. Hershan.

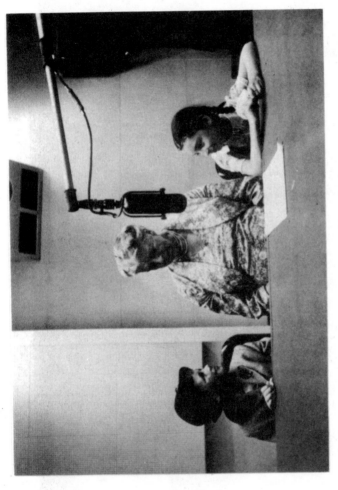

Mrs. Roosevelt with two young friends taping the record "Hello World!" "Hello World!" had its world premier at the opening of the Young People's Concerts of the Little Orchestra Society on November 10, 1956. Photo from the collection of Stella K. Hershan.

Eleanor with boxer Floyd Patterson, January 1962. Eleanor developed a warm relationship with Patterson. Photo from the collection of Stella K. Hershan.

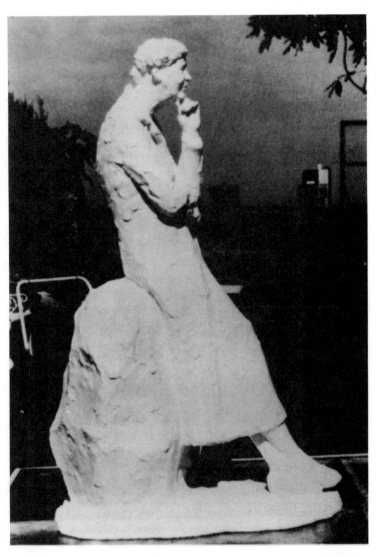

Sculpture of Eleanor by Penelope Jencks for the Eleanor Roosevelt monument at 72nd Street and Riverside Park in Manhattan. Photo by Hely Lima; used with permission of the photographer.

Part II _____

Perceptions of
Eleanor Roosevelt

Val-Kill

Hyde Park, New York, October 11, 1984. A sea of red, white, and blue balloons are dancing in the gentle autumn breeze. Golden leaves are falling into the spring-fed pond where a duck family waddles along, undisturbed by the sounds of the high school band playing "Beautiful Dreamer," Mrs. Roosevelt's favorite song. Eleanor Roosevelt used to like parties — not necessarily her own — but this, her one hundredth birthday party, would have pleased her. After all, she was getting her biggest wish. Val-Kill, the house she always considered her only real home, was being returned to her!

It all began sixty years before, in August 1924. Eleanor, her family, and her friends Nancy Cook and Marion Dickerman were enjoying their last picnic of the season at their favorite spot by a stream called Fall-Kill. Noticing how sad the women were about not being able to return that year, for Sara was closing the big house for the winter, Franklin offered them a few acres on the Roosevelt estate for their lifetime use to build a cottage of their own.

Franklin himself helped architect Henry Toombs design the structure in Dutch colonial style. By 1925 a small fieldstone house stood on the site, christened Val-Kill after the nearby stream. Nan and Marion moved into the cottage immediately, making it their permanent residence until 1947. Eleanor joined them on weekends and holidays during the summer. Here at last was a place she did not have to ask her mother-in-law's permission to invite friends. She had a house of her own! A place where she could be alone.

In 1927, Franklin and Eleanor became concerned about the many young people in Hyde Park and nearby rural areas who could not find work. Nancy Cook, who had taught handicrafts, suggested they set up a shop reproducing early American furniture and teach local men the skills. Eleanor thought this was a good idea and went to New York in search of a craftsman who could serve as a teacher. At a vocational school of which she was a trustee in Greenwich Village, she found Frank Landolfa.

Landolfa came to America from Bari, Italy, in 1924. He was only twenty-one years old, and his father, a fine furniture maker, had sent him to the United States in order to try to import their work there. But work was hard to come by, and greatly discouraged and disappointed by 1927, Frank decided to go back home.

When, just about this time, Eleanor Roosevelt appeared and invited him to come to Val-Kill, Frank was reluctant. But Eleanor decided he was just the right person to work at Val-Kill Industries. She found him a place to stay with a nice Italian family in Hyde Park; she encouraged him to go to the local dances — at one of which he met Rose. Rose had come to America with her parents when she was only five years old. Frank introduced her to Mrs. Roosevelt. "Rose is such a nice girl," Mrs. Roosevelt kept telling Frank. "I think you should settle down and start a family."

"Mrs. Roosevelt pushed me into marrying her," said Frank Landolfa some fifty years later, as he stood in the workshop of his one-hundred-year-old house in neighboring Poughkeepsie. On the wall behind him was a photograph of a slender, young Eleanor, peering seriously over Frank's shoulder while he worked on the leg of a table. Frank winked at the picture. About eighty years old, Frank was still debonair, a quick, wiry man with his cap at a rakish angle.

"Mrs. Roosevelt always tried to help us," Rose added with her quiet smile. "She gave us two antique chairs as a wedding present. Frank restored them. She always gave us presents when the children were born."

Frank motioned to another picture on the wall: an older, proud-looking woman, Sara Delano Roosevelt. "Frank got along so well with her," said Rose. "She was a real nice lady. Even spoke a little Italian. The Delanos had some Italian roots. My husband worked in the furniture factory for ten years. Things went well at first. The shop became too small, and several additions were built onto the factory. Later, a separate two-story building was added on. Frank made all the furniture for the president's cottage in Warm Springs, Georgia. More workers were hired, but no one could really help Frank. Only *he* did things right. He has not changed much." Frank grinned and nodded.

Still, the factory failed in the end, as times were very hard. "By that time we had bought this house," Rose said. "We had two small children. Mrs. Roosevelt found a job for Frank for six months, but after that, she said, he would have to be on his own. Jobs were just impossible to find. Frank finally decided to work for himself."[1]

After the collapse of the furniture enterprise, Eleanor Roosevelt bought out her two friends and converted the building into two apartments, one for herself and the other for her secretary, Malvina Thompson, fondly called "Tommy" by the entire family. A few guest rooms were also added for visitors for whom no space could be found at the "Big House." Plus, a swimming pool was installed for Franklin. Winston Churchill puffed his ever-present cigars at Val-Kill. Queen Wilhelmina of the Netherlands enjoyed the hot dogs grilled on the outdoor fireplace.

For Eleanor Roosevelt, Val-Kill became "my home" in Hyde Park after the death of the president. Among her visitors were Nikita Khrushchev, Marshal Tito, Haile Selassie, Jawaharlal Nehru, and John F. Kennedy. Every summer, she invited more than one hundred boys from the local Wiltwick School for delinquent youngsters, a project which was particularly close to her heart, for an outing. In the summer heat she would stand next to the grill, buttering rolls for her young guests.

"Mrs. Roosevelt," Dr. Ernst Papanek, the director of the school, would plead with her, "please, do not work so hard! The boys will eat those rolls even if they are not buttered!" "I buttered the rolls for the King and Queen of England," Eleanor Roosevelt would reply. "There is no reason that I should not do the same for these boys."[2]

Eleanor Roosevelt loved Christmas and the chance to give. All year long, guests at Val-Kill were asked to please help wrap the presents she had collected throughout her extended travels all over the world. The wrapped presents were then carefully marked and stored in a large hall closet which, from bottom to ceiling, was overflowing.

Beginning in 1935, Mrs. Roosevelt kept an exact list of her gifts. The family received practical presents. In 1935, Franklin D. Roosevelt, Jr., received six handkerchiefs, two pairs of pajamas, a daybed, and books. Daughter Anna received sheets and an old silver sugar bowl in 1940, but in 1938 she had received a fur jacket and a sofa. Grandchildren mostly got Junior League subscriptions and sometimes a check for five dollars. Secretary Morgenthau received six desk pads, an ashtray, a knife, and a matchbox in 1937, but in 1940 he received a picnic wagon. Queen Elizabeth, the Queen Mother, Prime Minister Nehru, and Madame Pandit received raisins, candied fruit, and maple sugar every year. Employees got turkeys, ties, and a check for twenty-five dollars.[3]

On Christmas Eve, Val-Kill usually had a number of overnight guests, and Mrs. Roosevelt was known to walk around the house in silent slippers to place stockings on each doorknob. Once, a guest hearing some noise got out of bed and curiously opened his door. Brusquely, the guest was ordered to "go back to bed" by an irritated Mrs. Roosevelt.

On Christmas Day, a long table was set for family and friends. A tree made out of bubble gum and surrounded by a green wreath provided the centerpiece. Next to each and every plate were small stacks of gaily wrapped special gifts. Place cards included little poems written for each guest by Eleanor herself, remembering a shared experience.

After the feast, which usually included roast turkey, everyone filed into the living room. A beautiful small tree from the Hyde Park grounds stood on a table. Each guest had a separate chair piled high with presents.

And Eleanor was known to wander around, urging the guests to please save paper and ribbon so that it could be used again next year, inquiring whether the gifts received were the right size, the right color, and just what everyone had wished for.

A long bench near the door was piled high with Eleanor's presents, and she was always the last person to open hers. Then she would ask someone to help her note down what and from whom she had received each item, so that she could write the proper thank-you note.

After the exchange of presents, Mrs. Roosevelt read Dickens's *Christmas Carol,* a custom which Franklin had started and which she faithfully continued. And just so that the holiday spirit was present even if nature failed to provide snow, Eleanor had pieces of cotton stuck on the windows of the cottage.

The hundreds of Christmas cards which Mrs. Roosevelt sent out each year were always personally signed by her. And, on Christmas 1962, one and a half months after her death, friends and family were still receiving Christmas gifts from Eleanor Roosevelt.[4]

Eleanor Roosevelt left Val-Kill to her children. Then, in 1970, it was sold to two real-estate developers for $225,000 to become a nursing home or senior-citizen community. Concerned citizens in Hyde Park, afraid that the development would damage a valuable historic asset, organized a drive to preserve the site. A town zoning ordinance prevented the developers from realizing their plan. Disappointed that they were now unable to turn a large profit, they converted Eleanor Roosevelt's home into four apartments and rented them out.

"This is Mrs. Roosevelt's living room," explained Barbara, a young woman who occupied Mrs. Roosevelt's apartment as she showed a visitor around. "And this is Mrs. Roosevelt's bedroom. Here is the porch where she likes to sleep when it is warm enough. She likes to hear the birds awakening and to see the ducks coming out on the pond."

Barbara stopped and chuckled a little. "We have been living here for one year now, but I always keep thinking of it as Mrs. Roosevelt's place. We have some closet doors which keep opening and closing. But I always tell my husband that it could not possibly be Mrs. Roosevelt. Eleanor Roosevelt would never ever disturb anyone!"[5]

It was an early summer morning in 1976 when Nancy Dubner, a young woman from Rochester, stood in the Rose Garden of the Roosevelt estate. Birds started to twitter lightly, and the rising sun painted pink the marble of the simple, square tombstone before her. "FRANKLIN DELANO ROOSEVELT 1882–1945," was engraved in the marble. President Roosevelt himself had designed the stone and specified that he wished to be buried in his own rose garden. And the only person he wanted beside him was his "Missus."

ANNA ELEANOR ROOSEVELT
1884–1962

Nancy gazed at the inscription. It had been twenty years before when, as a young student, she had met Mrs. Roosevelt at the American Association for the United Nations, when Mrs. Roosevelt had sat down on the floor with the young students and listened to what they had to say. Many things were on Nancy Dubner's mind that morning. She was still very involved in the women's movement and was president of the Women's Political Caucus. She wanted to tell Mrs. Roosevelt of her conviction that unless women got into the mainstream of American politics, they would not get equality. She wanted to tell her that if other first ladies had emulated her style, they would not have such a big battle now. "What can we do?" Nancy Dubner asked Mrs. Roosevelt silently, "what can we do that our voices will be heard?"

Suddenly she heard a voice. "Nancy." It was Mrs. Roosevelt! It had to be! She pronounced Nancy's name with a broad A, just as she had so long ago. "Nancy, I want you to get Val-Kill back for me. Get it back and make something out of it. Not a museum where people tip-toe around, but a place where people like you will meet, hold seminars, try to make the world a better place to live in."

Nancy drove the narrow, unmarked country road leading to Val-Kill, where tall trees cast long shadows on the hidden valley. Nancy got out of her car and stared. This was the home of Eleanor Roosevelt? These two dismal, gray, dilapidated shacks? Those were the grounds where people famous the world over had picnicked? Why, those grounds were littered with garbage!

Disconsolate, Nancy drove back to Rochester, but in her mind she kept hearing that voice: "Nancy, I want you to get Val-Kill back for me."

"What can *I* do?" Nancy replied silently and somewhat defiantly. "I am only one person! I cannot possibly get Val-Kill back." But the voice kept nudging her.

On the following day, Nancy wrote to Jonathan Bingham and Henry Jackson, who were in charge of the House Subcommittee on Parks and chairmen of the Senate Interior Committee. In her letter, she suggested that they include Val-Kill in the Roosevelt site that had been given to the National Park Department after the death of President Roosevelt. Copies of her letter were sent to the National Park Service to inquire what they thought of the idea. It was the time of the Gerald Ford administration, and the park department historian replied that "Mrs. Roosevelt's position in history is not quite clear."

Next, Nancy Dubner tried Orin Lehman at the State Department. Lehman had loved Eleanor Roosevelt, and he replied at once, "We'll do it!" But, as it turned out, the Park Department had financial difficulties.

Becoming more and more involved in that matter, Nancy found out about a women's group in Hyde Park, a private, nonprofit organization attempting to save Eleanor Roosevelt's former home. Then, Nancy heard that the actress Jean Stapleton had been at the FDR Library in Hyde Park doing research for a film in which she was to portray Mrs. Roosevelt. Nancy got in touch with Ms. Stapleton, who had also been terribly distressed when she had seen the awful condition of Val-Kill. She at once pledged to support Nancy's endeavor.

It had been in the 1950s when Eleanor Roosevelt had come backstage to meet the cast of *Come Back, Little Sheba,* in which Ms. Stapleton played in Chicago. "A light seemed to emanate from her," remembered Ms. Stapleton. "The entire cast was awed and no one could say a word. There was this radiantly beautiful woman making small talk with us." Many years later, Jean Stapleton was to play Eleanor Roosevelt in a television movie entitled "First Lady of the World," concentrating on the years when Mrs. Roosevelt served as a delegate to the United Nations General Assembly and was instrumental in the writing and passage of the Universal Declaration of Human Rights.

The first bill introduced to Congress on behalf of Val-Kill was rejected. The administration was still Republican. In 1977, Democrat Jimmy Carter became president, and the group of women tried again to contact Washington. A twelve-minute monologue was written by Rhoda Lerman in which Ms. Stapleton as Eleanor Roosevelt discussed her feelings for Val-Kill. The monologue was called "Soul of Iron."

A new hearing was held in the Senate. Nancy Dubner was there, as was former New York Senator Jacob K. Javits, who spoke of growing up on the Lower East Side of Manhattan when Eleanor Roosevelt taught at the settlement houses.

"Mrs. Roosevelt taught us boys how to take a bath," Javits recalled. "She really did! She spoke to us about the importance of cleanliness, and she literally showed us what to do in the local bathhouses."[6]

"Soul of Iron" was shown as Ms. Stapleton's and Ms. Lerman's testimony at that Senate hearing. "I received approval and glowing reviews from Mrs. Roosevelt's chauffeur, Tubby, and many other of her friends," said Ms. Stapleton.[7]

The bill making Val-Kill a national historic site was approved. The government offered the two real-estate entrepreneurs $300,000 to buy them out, but they had put the property on the market already. For them it had been a white elephant, but now, aware of the government's interest in it, their price went up to $1 million. "We have been offered $1.2 million!" they protested. "With just the building and the land, it's worth several times $300,000. The historic value alone should bring it up to 1 million!" The government retained an objective appraiser, who confirmed the value at $300,000.

The property was condemned because of its decayed condition, and the government took it over for $300,000 with plans to make it a national historic site. The developers sued the government. After a two-week trial in Manhattan, a jury upheld the appraisal at $300,000. The developers appealed. They lost again.

Work on the restoration began, with Emily L. Wright, a park ranger historian, hired to oversee the work. She was commissioned to do a report on the furniture and was in charge of tracing those pieces that had been auctioned off after Mrs. Roosevelt's death. How did Emily feel about coming so close to Mrs. Roosevelt?

"My father used to refer to Mrs. Roosevelt as 'that terrible woman!' "
Emily laughed. "He was a staunch Republican. But through my work
here I have come to really know Mrs. Roosevelt. It is almost as if I were
newly born."[8]

The work on the restoration took seven years, but on October 11,
1984, Eleanor had her house back. When President Carter signed the
bill creating the Eleanor Roosevelt National Historic Site," it was "in
order to commemorate for the education, inspiration and benefit of
present and future generations the life and work of an outstanding
woman in American History."

Franceska Macsali is the supervisory park ranger at the Roosevelt
sites. A local young woman, she had studied to become a teacher, but
with jobs not readily available in the public school system, she started to
work at the Franklin D. Roosevelt and Vanderbilt Mansion National
Historic Sites, which are within two miles of Val-Kill.

"During the first two years I worked at the home of President
Roosevelt, I read many books about the Roosevelt era," remembers
Franceska.

> I came to admire and love Eleanor Roosevelt. Here was a woman
> who had such an unhappy and lonely childhood and so many di-
> sasters happening later in her life, such as her husband becoming
> paralyzed from polio and never again able to walk, yet she never
> turned her back on life, never felt sorry for herself. Instead, she
> reached out to others who needed help—the poor, the downtrod-
> den. How much I wished to work at Val-Kill, the site dedicated to
> Eleanor Roosevelt!

Then, in 1982, Franceska was appointed the permanent park ranger
there. The site was scheduled to open on the hundredth anniversary of
the birth of Eleanor Roosevelt, October 11, 1984.

"The biggest problem for the park service was to find and acquire the
original furnishings in Mrs. Roosevelt's home," Francesca tells.

> When Val-kill was sold in 1970, all the furnishings had been sold
> at a public auction. Ever since 1977, when the government bought
> back the property, a search went on for those furnishings. It was
> difficult. Many people had died, others had moved away, and
> some others still did not want to part with any of the pieces for

sentimental reasons. Though some of the original furniture was finally found, the park service decided to purchase furnishings that matched those that were original to the house. It was very fortunate that, a few days after the death of Mrs. Roosevelt, a photographer from the FDR Library took interior photographs of the entire home. From these photographs we were able to restore Eleanor Roosevelt's home to the way it was during her lifetime.

Franceska personally helped carry in furnishings and placed them in their proper places. Fortunately, the many, many photographs Mrs. Roosevelt had of family and friends were in storage in the FDR Library. Placing those photographs in the right places in the twenty rooms of the home was also a job given to Franceska. She assisted Emily Wright, who was the historian and later site supervisor at Val-Kill. She helped to prepare the interpretive programs to acquaint visitors with the story of Eleanor Roosevelt's life and home.

"During the summers of 1982 and 1983," Franceska recalls,

we set up limited tours through the empty rooms, but showed a ten-minute slide program as a preview of what was to come later. It was possible to make Mrs. Roosevelt's story come to life by just concentrating on her as a person and telling stories about the house and her life there.

"I could actually see what her home was like and what kind of a person she was," I was once told by a man, and only later realized that he was blind.

Today, we show visitors to Val-Kill a twenty-minute orientation film, an overview of Eleanor Roosevelt's life from birth to death and also the history of the site. Emily and I assisted in the production of the film, editing the script and choosing some photographs. The FDR Library has roughly ten thousand photographs of Mrs. Roosevelt, and it took me several weeks to look through all of them. I did it twice and still found photos I had overlooked at first. We also worked on the site brochures and slide programs that were sent out to organizations interested in Val-Kill.

A great many details are involved in getting a park ready to be opened to the visiting public. The buildings and the grounds have to be restored to their historic appearance. In the case of Val-Kill it was especially difficult because the buildings had been privately owned and had been converted into individual apartments which were rented out. Now, paint samples had to be done so that the rooms could be repainted in the same colors they were during the historic period. Light fixtures had to be replaced, heating systems changed. It was fortunate that Mrs. Roosevelt had saved all her documents, including bills and check stubs. It all was stored in the FDR Library, and from those bills we were able to find out whether the roof of Mrs. Roosevelt's home was cedar or asphalt.

To see the buildings begin to take shape and to appear the way they had been in the historic past was a great thrill, Franceska recalls "What excitement when we were able to walk from one wing of Mrs. Roosevelt's home to the other!"

During the rental period, the two wings had been separated by walls. Once those walls came crashing down, the entire cottage was one again! And then came the day when all the park rangers carried in tables, chairs, chests of drawers, knick-knacks, and books. "Why, it looks just like it did when Mrs. Roosevelt invited me here!" one of the first visitors exclaimed upon entering, and he could not have pleased the staff more.

Nine years have passed since Val-Kill was opened to the public. Now, 32,000 visitors come to the home in any given year: from all parts of the United States, from Europe. A film was made there recently which will be shown in schools in Austria.

It was Franceska's idea to re-create Eleanor Roosevelt's Christmas. With the help of two seasonal employees, Sonia Hurley and Dorothy Barson, Val-Kill is decorated during the month of December exactly the way it was when Mrs. Roosevelt celebrated her favorite holiday there. And just in case nature does not provide the necessary snow, Franceska never forgets to tape cotton onto the windows, just as Mrs. Roosevelt had done.

"I have been at Hyde Park twelve years now, and the work has changed my life," says Franceska Macsali.

> I used to be shy, and it was difficult for me to express my dissatis-
> faction over things I found wrong. But now, after being aware of
> what Mrs. Roosevelt had done, I force myself to speak up. If I feel
> very strongly about an injustice or unfairness in our country, I
> write a letter. I had always thought it was easier to remain silent,
> but now I know that the difficult ways are the easy ones. To keep
> silent has become difficult for me. Val-Kill and getting to know
> Eleanor Roosevelt does that to you. And once you have found your
> way to Val-Kill, it will be difficult not to come back.[9]

The Big House

"This was my mother-in-law's house," visitors to the Roosevelt mansion in Hyde Park hear on their earphones, as the voice of Eleanor Roosevelt on tape leads them through the house. Indeed, this was the house of Sara Delano Roosevelt, and she never permitted anyone to forget it.

"Mama," Mrs. James Delano Roosevelt II, was born on September 21, 1854, at Algonac near Newburgh, New York, on the Hudson River. She was the seventh child of eleven — six boys and five girls. Her parents wanted to call her Sarah Philippa for Philippe De La Noye, the founder of the Delano family who arrived in Plymouth in 1621, but it seemed too big a name for a little girl, so they finally settled on Sarah, which soon became Sally. Her father was Warren Delano II, son of Warren Delano, a sea captain of Fairhaven, Massachusetts. By 1854, he was already a wealthy man. Having grown up in the days of clipper ships and whalers, he had followed his father to sea and built one of the most powerful and successful tea-export firms in the Orient. In 1843, he married Catherine Lyman of Northhampton. She was eighteen and he, thirty-three. Immediately after the wedding, Warren took his young bride back to Hong Kong. After three years they returned and eight years later settled in a large home in the Hudson River Valley.

It was a fine house of forty rooms, and it was there that Sally was born. She had a nurse, Mary Bell, sisters and brothers to play with, and many aunts and uncles.

In the fall of 1857, a great depression descended upon America. On October 23, eighteen New York banks suspended payments to their depositors, and others from Maine to California followed suit. But Warren Delano, in addition to his profitable Oriental tea trade and his ships, which were the envy of the maritime world, had since his return from China acquired real estate in New York City, as well as coal mines in Tennessee and other mining interests. His fortune had been estimated at close to a million dollars. He was generally thought of as one of the most successful businessmen of his day. So the Delanos, in spite of the depression, were not impoverished, yet they tried to sell their estate, Algonac. No one could afford it, much less maintain it.

At the age of fifty, Warren Delano decided to start anew. Leaving his wife and children behind, he sailed back to China and once more began to build up his business in Hong Kong. After two years, in 1862, Warren Delano brought his entire family, including a nanny, an English nurse, and a maid, to a great house called Rose Hill. It was to be their Chinese home.

The children had a large schoolroom with a view into gardens with palm trees and other tropical plants. "Papa," as Sally called her adored father, made them study French and music; he gave them a little pony carriage with straight-backed seats because he did not allow his children to slump. (This might account for Sara Roosevelt's later days' erect posture.) They dined at the home of one of their father's great Chinese friends. "Papa told us to pretend we liked the Chinese food though it was very strange to us," Sara recalled years later, but she also remembered that it had been served on magnificent china and silver.

But there were no Christmas trees and no snow, and the semitropical climate of Hong Kong was not good for the children's health. The four older children were sent home, and by 1886, Mr. Delano's financial situation had improved enough for all of them to return to the United States. Since Algonac had been rented out, he decided to take his family to Europe until they could settle down again in the Hudson Valley.

They spent the first year in an apartment in Paris. Sally, twelve years old now, spoke French fluently. During her years in Europe she added German and became quite comfortable in European culture, very knowledgeable about classical arts and music.

After eight years the Delanos came back home to the Algonac estate. Sally played piano for her parents' guests, went horseback riding, and helped her mother entertain. Of course there were many parties, picnics, and dances. "Papa" looked over his daughters' beaux and firmly indicated if he did not approve. The Delanos, after all, belonged to what was considered the best society in New York.

In 1880, Sally, now twenty-five years old, tall and slim with classical features and dark hair and eyes, met James Roosevelt, a widower twenty-five years older than she. James was a seventh-generation Roosevelt, an imposing, handsome man with muttonchop whiskers. His first wife, Rebecca Howland, had died in 1876 and left him one son, James Roosevelt Roosevelt, called Rosy. James Roosevelt bred trotters, hunted, and decided who belonged in New York society. As president of a small railroad, he traveled in his own private car. Though he was a Democrat, he thought that politics were not quite "gentlemanly." It was this man whom Sally Delano decided was to be her husband.

Warren Delano was not quite pleased that his daughter wished to marry a man twice her age, although he otherwise approved of James Roosevelt. The wedding took place on October 7, 1880. On January 30, 1882, Sally bore him a son, whom they named Franklin Delano. On December 8, 1900, James Roosevelt died, and eighteen-year-old Franklin became the only man in his widowed mother's life.

The Roosevelt mansion in Hyde Park was home to Franklin for as long as he lived. It was the place where he was born, where he grew up, where his children grew up. From here he started his political career, and after 1921, when he became ill with infantile paralysis, he spent much time there. He loved the beautiful view from his balcony of the Hudson River, changing with the seasons. After 1933, when Franklin became president, he called it his "Summer White House." There, on June 20, 1942, the president and British Prime Minister Winston Churchill signed the agreement to build the world's first atomic bomb. From his office there, on November 6, 1944, Franklin broadcast his last campaign speech, which led to his fourth term. In his will, he left the place to his wife and children, but he also left a private letter to Eleanor, saying that he did not think they could afford to run it, and advising her and the children to give the house to the government at once. They all agreed.[1]

The secretary of the Interior accepted the title to the estate on November 21, 1945, when Mrs. Roosevelt and her children waived their interests in the house and grounds. The site was formally dedicated on April 12, 1946, on the first anniversary of the president's death.

Next to the house is the Franklin D. Roosevelt Library, administered by the National Archives and Record Service. The museum section duplicates the president's study, with his ship models, gifts from foreign rulers, and special exhibits about the lives and careers of Franklin and Eleanor.

Every year, thousands upon thousands of people from all over the world come to visit the Roosevelt home, to wander through the grounds' magnificent tall trees, to go from room to room and be made to feel that they are personal guests of the Roosevelt family.

To the visitors in 1952, the Roosevelt home became "Harold's House." In that year, Harold Kenneth Nelson became site specialist of the Franklin D. Roosevelt National Historic Site. A tall handsome man in his park service uniform, Harold actually looked like a Roosevelt. Seeing him standing there at the door with his warm, welcoming smile, visitors often appeared startled. Could it be a Roosevelt? one could almost see them thinking as he took their admission tickets. In the entrance hall, Harold usually gathered the visitors around him. "The Roosevelt kids always left all their junk here," he would say as he pointed to a massive oak wardrobe. "Tennis rackets, ice skates, whatever they just had been using. It was too much trouble for them to carry it all to their rooms. Often they would come in from horseback riding to the dinner table, and Mrs. James Roosevelt would sniff a little and say, 'Do I smell horses?' "

Harold was especially interested in the children the visitors brought along. He would point out to them a large china cat seated in the living room. Mrs. Roosevelt had once given that cat away, Harold told his young audience, but later she missed her and asked for her back. "Eleanor Roosevelt always had time for people," he would reminisce. "She used to treat me not as a park department employee, but more like a friend. Once she asked me to be personal escort to Princess Beatrix of the Netherlands, who now is Queen."

The children always wanted to hear stories about Fala, President Roosevelt's little black Scottish terrier. Fala always traveled with the president—even to his inaugurations—and Fala is now buried in the Rose Garden behind the graves of Eleanor and Franklin.

"There is a romance between myself and my work," Harold often told the visitors. "I want to be here. This is my house. It is my home for eight hours every day. And here Eleanor Roosevelt is alive for me. Just knowing her made you a better person. I felt that she was a personal friend of mine. She was such a beautiful woman, with a beauty that was inside of her. She was real tall, as tall as I am, and quite thin. And she cared about children so much—especially handicapped and retarded children."

Upstairs, visitors saw the room in which Franklin Roosevelt had been born, his boyhood room, the president's room with the closet door open and inside: the dark cape and fedora he wore during his last campaign; his wheelchair (which was just an ordinary chair transformed according to his specifications); and on a soft club chair, Fala's collar and leash.

Sometimes, Harold would take special visitors to the third floor, to the rooms where the Roosevelt children used to live: large, light, with many beds and a round chamber pot beneath each one of them.

Harold would also tell visitors about the many famous guests who had come to Hyde Park. "Now there was big excitement when Mr. Khrushchev and his wife came here from Russia," he remembered. "They both could not speak English at all, but they sure smiled a lot. I think that Mrs. Roosevelt took them for tea and cookies over to her own home."

"Her own home?" Visitors would ask puzzled. "Wasn't this her home?"

"No," Harold would reply slowly and thoughtfully, shaking his head. "Eleanor Roosevelt lived here and she raised her family here, but it was not *her* home. It was her mother-in-law's home. And, being the considerate person she was, Eleanor Roosevelt always respected this."[2]

Harold Nelson was in government service for thirty-three years. Before he came to work for the park department, he was a deputy sheriff of Dutchess County and a baker and cook in the Coast Guards. "Nelson would have someone smiling within a minute," said Bill Hubbard, chief of visitor services at the Roosevelt home. "Harold was always an example for new employees. His enthusiasm and love for the FDR home and the people who used to live there infected those of whom he was in charge. Harold loved people, all people, but he especially loved children, animals, and nature."

Twice a month during the school year, Harold gave a course at a Hyde Park elementary school and at the Regina Coeli school. He called it "Happenings in Nature." "Go hug a tree and listen to its heart!" he told his class of first-graders. "The bark of a tree is like the skin of people, and woodpeckers are to trees what dentists are to people because they remove the dead material from the trees. Trees are like mothers to animals because they feed, house, and protect them. It takes seventy-eight trees to keep each one of us alive with oxygen."

Harold's great love for animals and nature is expressed in his own drawings of birds, flowers, fruit, and trees in "Woods Trails," a teacher's guide to the Environment Study Area. "Harold would never even kill a rattlesnake!" said Ellie, Harold's wife. "Harold was the kindest man I have ever known," said Mary McClure, a tall, silver-haired lady who had worked alongside him for many years. "The Roosevelt house will never be the same without him."[3]

On July 12, 1981, Harold died of a heart attack. He was fifty-eight years old and had worked almost to the hour of his death in the house he so loved. On June 18, 1982, the park service planted a tree for him at the Regina Coeli school. Attached to it is a plaque which reads: "In memory of Harold Nelson for his years of dedicated services to the children of the Regina Coeli College to Children."

MORE STORIES FROM THE BIG HOUSE

"We were only six state troopers stationed at Hyde Park," related one trooper, who was just about twenty years old when he was assigned to guard the Roosevelt mansion and the president himself whenever he was in Hyde Park. The years were 1942 to 1945, the time of World War II.

When the president came from Washington two of us were sent to the mansion to guard him. It was kind of ridiculous. There are those big grounds with lots of shrubbery. If someone had wanted to kill the president, he could easily have hidden out there. There was practically no security at all to guard the president's life. A wooden ladder went up to his bedroom window. In case of a fire, a trooper was supposed to help him down. How? The president was paralyzed. No way could he walk! And he was a big man, too. No trooper could have carried him down that wooden ladder. But fortunately nothing ever happened.

The biggest excitement I can remember was one night when a spotlight was suddenly turned on the mansion from a boat on the river. The Coast Guards came rushing along, and it turned out that some fellow, a dentist from New York, was taking his girlfriend on a ride on the Hudson, and in order to show her the house where the president lived, he turned on the spotlight. Well, those two were scared all right when they caused all that commotion. Another time I was standing on guard and something was rustling in the bushes. I quickly pulled out my gun and yelled, "Who's there?" A little kid came crawling out, a nine- or ten-year-old boy who had run away from home. His parents came to pick him up.

It was kind of dull being a guard there. Among the troopers and the people who ran the mansion it was sort of understood that we could come into the kitchen and help ourselves to a glass of milk or some of the goodies they had in the refrigerator. Someone must have complained. Once, when FDR was in the house and we came into the kitchen, there was this great big padlock on the refrigerator door. Now Eleanor would never have put it there. She was much too considerate, the most considerate person I had ever known.

No one was supposed to know when the president was coming up to Hyde Park from Washington, but all of Poughkeepsie knew at once when he was expected. Great quantities of meat were ordered at the butcher, and once he knew, everyone knew. Eighty thousand people knew! FDR liked to play little tricks on the security people. He had this little car with hand controls. It is standing in the FDR Library now. He used to zoom with it through the fields, and the security people had to scramble to keep up with him.

People respected him a great deal, though. No photographs were taken without him knowing, just when he posed and smiled, sometimes even while he was adjusting his braces. People were not even aware that the security people always had to carry him to his car. By himself, he could not walk a single step. The president could not walk, yet he made an entire country get on its feet again.

FDR was a father much like any other father. Franklin, Jr., was home from college one day and was having a party. The kids were drinking beer and dancing and carrying on. The president was upstairs in his bedroom and could not get any sleep, so he was pounding on the floor with his cane. I tried to hush the young people, but they did not pay any attention. It was quite incredible. Here was the president of the United States, the most important man in the world with a war going on, and, just like any other father, he could not control his kids!

Toward the end of the war, we, the troopers kept guessing how much longer it was going to last. We slept in barracks—it was just like being in the army—and we heard rumors that the Germans were flying Hitler over to Hyde Park to surrender himself. Just about that time, on a very dreary morning, we were called out at five o'clock in the morning to guard the president. He was going to drive out—at five o'clock in the morning! We were bursting with curiosity, but all that we were told was to report to the mansion at once. Just as we got there, FDR was being carried to his car. With him was a stranger, a little man with a dark hat pulled down over his ears and a dark coat. "That's it!" we whispered to each other. That man was the contact.

The president's car drove off and we followed. It still was dark. The car went north, up to Tarrytown. At the railroad tracks it came to a halt. We jumped out. The security people carried the president up along the railroad tracks. The little man in his dark hat and coat walked beside him. Everything was so still that we barely dared to whisper to each other. Perhaps they were bringing Hitler here by special train, we guessed. The president stood quietly on his crutches. Slowly it was getting light. Some birds began to twitter. That was it, someone told us. That little man with the dark hat was from the Audubon Society. He was to show the president how thousands of some special birds took off at sunrise. We burst out laughing. The president turned and shook his fists at us, warning us to be quiet. But the angrier he got the louder we laughed, and of course the birds never showed up. It was all so long ago.

Just a few months ago my grandson said to me, "Hey, you always tell us about Hyde Park, Grandpa. Can't we go there sometimes?" And I thought, yeah, why don't we do that? So, my wife and I and my daughter and her husband and the kids drove up there.

As we walked around the grounds, a young woman came up to me and asked me whether I had been to Hyde Park before. I told her that I had been there in 1943. She looked at me kind of puzzled. "But we didn't have it in 1943," she said. "That's right," I told her. "The president had it at that time." She looked at me and shook her head. Then she said, "Oh."[4]

One of the park ranger historians and interpreters taking visitors around and talking to them is Haywood Smith. His face lights up with a big smile when he talks of the history of the Roosevelt mansion and of the people who used to live there.

Haywood came to Hyde Park in January 1981. He had studied history at Marist College in Hyde Park and heard of an opening for an interpreter at the home. He was introduced to his work by Harold Nelson.

"I was so fortunate that I still had the opportunity to know him," said Haywood. "Harold was never negative about anything. He was for the team. He loved animals and he loved young people. He certainly loved Eleanor Roosevelt. He conveyed this love to me and gave me a real feeling for her, even though I never knew her when she was alive."[5]

Haywood Smith and, in fact, everyone else in Hyde Park were glad that neither Eleanor Roosevelt nor Harold Nelson were still alive when tragedy struck the Roosevelt mansion in the early hours of January 23, 1982.

"The alarm went off at 12:12 A.M.," wrote Emily Wright, park ranger historian.

As soon as the Hyde Park volunteer fire department arrived and verified the existence of a fire, one of the park supervisors began calling employees who lived nearby. "Get there quickly to save the artifacts!" By 1:15 A.M. nearly twenty-five park employees were gathered there at the home. The scene was awesome. Lights from the fire trucks lit up the front of the building like a stage setting. Every detail of the façade was visible in the strong light. But illumination was unnecessary for seeing the twenty to thirty foot flames leaping from the roof over the entire section. Dazed and bewildered and unbelieving we watched the flames, the fire fighters on ladders, and waited for someone to tell us what to do. The park museum specialist ran out the front door. Bent over from coughing from the smoke, he still managed to talk the fire fighters into letting us enter the building. He and several of the other staff members had been in the home for nearly thirty minutes trying to rescue furnishings in the most important rooms in the second floor, the President's birthroom and boyhood room, his adult bedroom and dressing room. But they needed a great deal more help.

Against their better judgment, the fire fighters agreed to let the remainder of the staff (with several spouses and friends) enter. Twenty-five people ran in the front door as a unit, no one giving thought to personal safety. The museum specialist took charge, yelling out orders of what class of objects to take out. Paintings and prints went first; small upholstered pieces and ceramics next. Draperies and other movable objects later. Really large pieces of furniture were pushed to the center of rooms and covered with tarpaulin. Conditions were incredible. The only light was coming in windows and doors from the fire trucks. Water was pouring down the walls and forming sheets in the doorways. As the water load built up on the second floor from 100,000 gallons used to put out the fire, ceilings on the first floor began to crack. We would look up to see a crack run ten to fifteen feet across the ceiling. A heavy ceramic chandelier in the Dresden Room of the main floor was causing added pressure on the ceiling. An employee miraculously took down the fixture in less than five minutes; normally the time involved would have been considerably more. Fire fighters still had to punch a small hole into the ceilings of several rooms to relieve the water load and prevent ceilings from collapse. Smoke never caused a visibility problem on the bottom floors since the fire was mostly contained above the second floor where the children's rooms used to be. But we could smell and feel the effect of the smoke. In addition, while we were running from the home to other buildings with furnishings, the temperature oscillated between 0 and 5 degrees. By 3:00 A.M., snow began to fall heavily.

The park rescue team was composed of people from all park divisions: administration, curatorial, visitor services and maintenance. It included the superintendent, office workers, housekeepers, interpreters, curators, supervisors, and maintenance workers of all types. Family and friends who aided in the effort included a nurse, housewives, a history professor, an IBM employee, and two teenagers. The volunteer fire department not only saved the building but assisted greatly in saving the furnishings. At least four of our staff were also fire fighters. In one instance, when park employees were finally told to leave the building, an interpreter from the home put his fire hat on again and went back in.

We emerged from this disaster in better shape than seemed possible. The building, though badly damaged, still stands and will be restored. No one was seriously injured or killed. Only a very few artifacts were lost; the most important pieces either escaped damage or can be restored.

Staff members who ran into the burning building to save the collection have been asked numerous times "Why did you do it?"

We have a variety of answers but all come down to one:

"It was our job. We are here to take care of the home of one of the most famous Presidents. Roosevelt loved his home in Hyde Park. Here we tell millions of visitors about FDR the President and the man. Without the home and the furnishings, the story would not be complete. On an even more personal level, most of us have grown to love the home. We have our favorite rooms, favorite objects, favorite anecdotes about it. There is also an element of pride in being in part responsible for the 'Home of Franklin Roosevelt.' "[6]

Chapter 7 ——————————————————

Victims of the Holocaust

DR. GISELLA PERL

The greatest crime in Auschwitz was to be pregnant. Dr. Gisella Perl, a Hungarian gynecologist who was both an inmate and physician at the concentration camp, realized that to save the lives of hundreds of pregnant women, she would have to prevent them from giving birth.[1]

"I met Mrs. Eleanor Roosevelt sometime in 1947," Dr. Perl related in her own words.

> I was brought from the horrible, horrible death camps Auschwitz and Bergen-Belsen to speak, to tell of the incredible physical and psychological tortures and deaths of the six million Jewish people by the Nazi empire. I was in New York for many months. It took me quite a time to adjust myself to the rich, free, beautiful life of the United States. I went on telling the unbelievable tragedy of the Jewish people, speaking in town after town, reliving all the horrors. I did not want to be a doctor anymore. I really could not be one. I had no papers in my hand proving my education nor my certificate that I was a doctor.
>
> One evening after my speech at the United Jewish Appeal, I was introduced to Mrs. Eleanor Roosevelt who was seated in the audience. She came to my table and told me: "Dr. Perl, stop torturing yourself. Be a doctor again. I would like to see you."
>
> I was still in a fog, I did not understand her simple, honest

words. But the next day I wrote a letter to her, asking for an appointment. Her answer came within a few days, inviting me for lunch at her home.

I don't remember the room, nor what I ate, because she radiated such love and understanding that nothing else was of importance to me. "Don't torture yourself any longer, become a doctor again," Mrs. Roosevelt repeated those unforgettable words.

But I am helpless, I answered. I have no papers, nothing. And then I began to tell Mrs. Roosevelt my story.

From the ghetto, they took me to the cattle wagons. They took everything away from me except the dress covering my body. Yet, I was able to hide in its bodice my greatest treasure. My diploma that stated that I was a physician. In Auschwitz, despite the dirt and the lice, that diploma remained hidden against my heart.

In the camp, Gisella Perl was chosen by Dr. Mengele as one of five doctors and four nurses to work in a hospital ward that had no beds, no bandages, no drugs, and no instruments. She tended to every disease caused by torture, starvation, filth, lice, and rats, to every bone broken or head cracked open by beating. She performed surgery without anesthesia on women whose breasts had been lacerated by whips and became infected. Dr. Perl had only one palliative, her voice. She told her patients stories, told them that one day they would all have birthdays again, that one day they all would sing again. Her boss was Josef Mengele, the "doctor of death" of Auschwitz, who performed brutal experiments on inmates, particularly women, the physically handicapped, and twins. It was Mengele who decided who would go to the gas chambers.

"Dr. Mengele told me that it was my duty to report every pregnant woman to him," Dr. Perl continued telling her story to Mrs. Roosevelt. "He said that they would go to another camp for better nutrition, even for milk. So, some women began to run directly to him, telling him that they were pregnant. They all were taken to the research block and used as guinea pigs. And finally two lives would be thrown into the crematorium. I decided that never again would there be a pregnant woman at Auschwitz."

Gisella Perl interrupted every pregnancy from then on during the night, on a dirt floor with only her dirty hands. "No one will ever know what it meant to me to destroy those babies," Dr. Perl said in the quiet of Eleanor Roosevelt's living room. "But if I had not done it, both mother and child would have been murdered."

On a cold winter day in January 1945, Dr. Mengele called Gisella Perl out from the "hospital." The Russian forces were approaching and the Germans were hastily shutting down the gas chambers and evacuating the camps. He told her that she was to leave immediately.

"Can I go with a friend?" Dr. Perl asked. The answer was no. "An S.S. soldier grabbed my arm and we went out from the gates of Auschwitz."

We walked many hours until we arrived at a railway station. A train was waiting. I did not dare to ask where we were going. I was certain some special torture and death was waiting for me. After many long hours the train stopped in Berlin. The S.S. soldier told me that we were changing trains. I asked permission to go to the toilet. He came with me and stood at the door. And now, shaking with fear, I finally took out from the bodice of my dress the tattered and torn paper. My diploma. I tore it into small pieces and flushed it down the toilet.

The next train took her to Hamburg and a camp nearby. From there, she was transferred to Bergen-Belsen. At the exact moment when the British troops were moving in to liberate Bergen-Belsen, Dr. Gisella Perl was delivering a baby, the first free child born there. She remained in the camp until fall, when she wandered throughout Germany on foot searching for her family. After nineteen days she learned that her husband had been beaten to death just before the liberation, and her teenage son, who had been taken from her when she was deported, had died in a gas chamber. Her strength finally left her and she tried to poison herself, but she was rescued and taken to a convent in France to recuperate.

"After I had finished telling my story," Dr. Perl related, "Mrs. Roosevelt stood up with tears streaming from her eyes, and said: 'I shall help you to be a doctor again. You will get your diploma.' Eleanor Roosevelt gave me hope and courage again."

Several weeks later, Congressman Sol Bloom called Dr. Perl to Washington. He told her that he had introduced a bill that granted her American citizenship. After a few more weeks she received her diploma as a physician.

In 1951, Dr. Perl opened an office in Manhattan. "I was the poorest doctor on Park Avenue," she said, "but I had the greatest practice. All the inmates of Auschwitz and Bergen-Belsen who had managed to survive were my patients."

Meanwhile, Dr. Perl also wrote her memoirs and sent the manuscript to Eleanor Roosevelt, thanking her for everything she had done for her. "My dear Dr. Perl," Mrs. Roosevelt wrote in reply, "this is an extraordinary, interesting and horrifying manuscript and I think it should not only be published but read by as many people as possible." Eleanor Roosevelt gave Dr. Perl permission to put those words into her book.

"Since the first day I met her till the last day of her life, my love and prayers always followed this great woman," wrote Dr. Perl.[2]

Later, Dr. Perl became a member of the staff of Mount Sinai Hospital and worked for Dr. Alan F. Gutmacher, chairman of obstetrics and gynecology. She delivered three thousand babies in New York and became an expert in treating infertility. In 1979, Dr. Perl decided to move to Israel, where she donated her time to the gynecological clinics of the Shaare Zedek Medical Center in Jerusalem. She lived there with her daughter, Gabriella, who had been hidden during the war years with a non-Jewish family, and a grandson.

In her seventies, Dr. Perl found, "It is worthwhile to live."[3]

ANNE FRANK

"Dear Sir," wrote Jennie C., a high school student at Peosta, Iowa, in October 1980, to the director of information at the Franklin D. Roosevelt Library in Hyde Park, New York. "I have just recently become interested in Anne Frank and her life. So I was hoping you might write me and answer some questions. I was wondering, since Mrs. Roosevelt wrote the introduction to Anne's Diary and was interested in the Franks, if maybe she knew them. If she did, maybe you could give me a little information about them from your point of view. Thank you for taking the time to read this."

Jenny's letter was only one of hundreds that come yearly to the library, inquiring about Anne's diary.

The Diary of a Young Girl first came to America in manuscript form in about 1948. A prominent literary agency which was headed by a Viennese emigré at once recognized its enormous value and world-wide potential and sent it to a major publishing house. There it landed on the desk of Mary C., a young editor fresh out of college. Tears rolling down her face after reading it, Mary wrote her report, stating her conviction that this story had enormous impact and was bound to become the book of the century. That report was sent on to her boss, the editor in chief.

"No," was his penciled reply on Mary's report. "The American public would not find this story of any interest." Mary asked a coworker to read the manuscript, and the response was identical to her own.

Mary marched into the office of her boss and asked to present her case at the monthly editorial board meeting. Amused by the innocent enthusiasm of this young employee, the editor in chief agreed to let her speak on behalf of Anne's diary. They listened to her politely but shook their heads. They agreed with their editor in chief. The publishing house sent the manuscript back to the literary agent with a form rejection slip.

In the years to follow, when the book went on its journey around the globe, Mary's editor in chief—to his credit—had her report framed and hung it on the wall in his office.[4]

The Diary of a Young Girl tells the story of the Frank family, who had emigrated from Frankfurt am Main to Amsterdam in 1933, the year Hitler became chancellor of Germany. On May 10, 1940, the Netherlands was abruptly attacked by German troops, and the Nazis began their persecution and deportation to extermination camps of the Jews in Holland.

In 1942, when the Franks' older daughter, Margot, received a deportation order for Germany, Otto Frank decided to move his family into hiding. A friend of his, Victor Kugler, an Austrian who had moved to Amsterdam after World War I, had a hidden apartment installed in his building at 263 Prinsengracht Street, the annex of his spice business. A narrow, ladder-like staircase led to a false bookcase which could only be opened from the inside. It was there that the Franks, together with another family, the Van Daans, whose young son, Peter, was also threatened with deportation, hid for two years. It was there that Anne wrote her diary.

On August 4, 1944, Karl Silberbauer, an Austrian S.S. man in Holland, was about to go to lunch when the telephone rang on his desk. The caller was a clerk from the Kugler spice house. He informed Silberbauer that Jews were hidden at Prinsengracht Street.

Postponing his lunch, Silberbauer stood up in his green uniform. The "green police" were the Germans in Holland who imposed a reign of terror. The Dutch froze at the sight of a "green policeman." Silberbauer rounded up a squad of men and drove with a police van, swastika flags flying, to the given address. The clerk was waiting for them. Silently he pointed his thumb upward.

With guns drawn the S.S. men stormed up the narrow staircase, removed the false bookcase, and found the hiding families. They were all arrested, all furniture and clothing confiscated. Only some books and papers were left scattered on the floor. Miep, a secretary in the firm who had taken care of the hidden Jewish people throughout the two years by bringing them food and everything else they needed, found a little note-book among those papers. It was Anne's diary.[5]

On September 3, 1944, on one of the last freight trains taking Jews out of Holland, the Franks were deported. On an unknown date in March 1945, Anne died of malnutrition, exposure, and typhus in Bergen-Belsen. She was fifteen years old. Otto Frank never again saw his family after their arrival in the concentration camps. He was taken to a men's camp at Auschwitz, where he performed forced labor, and was freed by the Russians in January 1945. He later remembered how the Russians had arrived, wearing snow-white fur coats. Searching for his family after he was liberated, Frank found out that he was the only one who had survived.

Back in Amsterdam, Miep handed him the diary of his daughter Anne. He decided that her memory had to be preserved when he read her closing words: "In spite of everything, I still believe that people are really good at heart." Six years later, after many American publishers had found Anne's diary unworthy of being published, Doubleday con-tracted it.

On April 22, 1952, in Eleanor Roosevelt's famous column, "My Day," that appeared in the papers, she wrote:

> Last winter in Paris I read the manuscript of a book, which I have just now received in bound form, called: "The Diary of a Young Girl" by Anne Frank. It is the story of a child who went through the invasion of Holland and all the fears that Jewish people had to live through at that time. The book tells us simply and vividly what it was like. I think it is well for us who have forgotten so much of that period to read about it now, just to remind ourselves that we never want to go through such things again if possible. Her story ended tragically. She died in the concentration camp at Bergen Belsen. This diary should teach us all the wisdom of pre-venting any kind of totalitarianism that could lead to oppression and suffering of this kind.[6]

Eleanor Roosevelt consented to write the book's introduction. It be-gins:

This is a remarkable book. Written by a young girl — and the young are not afraid of telling the truth — it is one of the wisest and most moving commentaries on war and the impact on human beings that I have ever read. Anne Frank's account of the changes wrought upon eight people hiding out from the Nazis for two years during the occupation of Holland, living in constant fear and isolation, imprisoned not only by the terrible outward circumstances of war but inwardly by themselves, made me shockingly, intimately aware of war's greatest evil — the degradation of the human spirit.[7]

"Dear Mrs. Roosevelt," wrote Otto Frank on March 25, 1952, "I just have to write to you and thank you from all my heart for the impressive introduction you wrote for my daughter Anne's Diary, for the help you are giving by your writing in spreading her ideals. I personally try to do everything to fulfill her testament, that only love and not hatred can build a better world."[8]

Later that year, Otto Frank came to New York, and Eleanor Roosevelt invited him for lunch in her apartment. She asked Mr. Frank many questions, wanted to know more about Anne and about the happenings after the family was arrested. She urged him to contact her again on his next visit to New York.

Six years later, at the beginning of 1958, Otto Frank did return to the United States. Again he was invited by Mrs. Roosevelt to her home. Otto Frank was troubled. Twentieth Century–Fox wanted to make a film based on the book. Would they do it justice? Would Hollywood turn it into something commercial? Eleanor Roosevelt agreed that they might, yet she also told him that many more people would be induced to read the book after having seen the film, and Anne's message would be spread around the world. The film was made.

A Broadway play, *The Diary of Anne Frank,* had opened on October 5, 1955. The diary had been published in over twenty countries.

On October 4, 1963, at eight o'clock in the morning as usual, Inspector Karl Silberbauer went to his job at a police station in Vienna. On his desk was a note ordering him to appear immediately before his superior at the local ministry.

Did he remember having arrested the Frank family in Amsterdam on August 4, 1944? What could he answer but, "Yes."

He was ordered to turn in his gun and police identification. Was he sorry about what had happened? Karl Silberbauer was asked later in an interview. Yes, of course he was sorry. Now, as a civilian, he had to pay the fare on the trolley car, and he had difficulties making the payments on his new furniture. Had he ever read the book by Anne Frank? Yes, but he was disappointed that his name was not even mentioned in it, for the diary had come to an end before the arrest.[9]

For Victor Kugler, the Christian who had provided sanctuary to Anne Frank, her family, and four other Jews, "Love thy neighbor" was not just a slogan. After the arrest of the Franks, he too was incarcerated for several months, then sent to a Dutch concentration camp. He died on December 17, 1981, at age eighty-one in Canada.

LION FEUCHTWANGER

On June 14, 1940, Hitler danced a little jig at the Arc de Triomphe in Paris. The red flag with the black swastika was hoisted on the Eiffel Tower.

Many of the German and Austrian writers who had fled the Nazis for political or religious reasons were now trapped in France. On June 22, France signed an armistice with Germany, and one of its clauses required that the government "surrender upon demand all Germans named by the Nazi occupation in France as well as in French possessions." The term "German" meant anyone from the "greater Reich," whether German, Austrian, Czechoslovakian, or Polish.

The world-famous writer Thomas Mann was first on Goebbel's wanted list, but Mann and part of his family were already safely in the United States. Still in France were his son, Golo, as well as his brother, the distinguished sixty-nine-year-old writer Heinrich Mann. Also trapped in France at that time were many other prominent European writers—among them, Franz Werfel and his wife, Alma Mahler Werfel, Herta Pauli, and the noted German Jew Lion Feuchtwanger and his wife, Marta.

Sometime in 1942, an emaciated Lion Feuchtwanger, dressed in rags, stood behind a barbed-wire fence in a detention camp in France. Someone on the outside spotted him and surreptitiously snapped a photo. It was smuggled into America and landed on a desk at the Viking Press, Feuchtwanger's American publisher. It was taken to Washington, to Eleanor Roosevelt.

Dorothy Thompson, the wife of Sinclair Lewis and herself a famous American publicist and journalist, was also a close friend of Eleanor

Roosevelt. She told Mrs. Roosevelt of the Emergency Rescue Committee which she and a group of other outstanding and concerned Americans had formed to rescue the writers. A meeting was arranged. Eleanor Roosevelt was informed that the American consulates in Vichy France had decided not to grant visas to refugees from Hitler because they did not wish to interfere between Vichy France and Germany. They also explained to Eleanor Roosevelt that to do so was equivalent to a death sentence.

Mrs. Roosevelt reported what she had learned to her husband. Soon afterward, FDR ordered the State Department to issue visitor's visas to "those of superior intellectual attainment, of indomitable spirit, experienced in vigorous support of the principles of liberal government and who are in danger of persecution or death at the hands of autocracy."

Eleanor made certain that this order was carried out. She reminded the officials at the State Department daily, urging them to hurry the most urgent cases. Mrs. Roosevelt's most important source of information concerning the would-be emigrés was Thomas Mann, but on at least one occasion, she took matters into her own hands.

Always an avid reader, she had been an admirer of the works of Lion Feuchtwanger for many years. Once, when he was ill with the flu during a lecture tour in the United States, Mrs. Roosevelt visited him in his hotel and later sent a signed photograph of herself to him in Berlin. (When the Nazis invaded the Feuchtwanger home, Marta Feuchtwanger recalled that they tore it from the wall, stamped on it, and cursed it.)

Aware that Feuchtwanger was in special danger because of his early anti-Nazi writings, Eleanor Roosevelt became impatient with the slow action displayed by the State Department under Cordell Hull. She appealed for help to her friend Dr. Fritchman, pastor of the Unitarian Church in Los Angeles, who in turn arranged for Waitstill Sharp, pastor of the Boston Unitarian Church, to travel immediately to Marseilles to aid the Feuchtwangers. By that time, Lion had been spirited out of the camp disguised as an old woman in a big coat and a kerchief.

It had been known that the prisoners usually were taken to wash in a nearby brook in the afternoon. Because they were in their underwear, security was not tight. An aide to the American consul in Marseilles snatched Feuchtwanger into his official car and disguised him as an old woman. When guards stopped them and asked who the old woman in the back was, they were told it was the aide's mother-in-law, ill with typhoid. They quickly waved them on.

As it was strictly forbidden for a diplomat to shelter someone wanted by the Nazis, the American consul put himself in grave danger. "It is terrible for me having to refuse all those poor people who line up daily by the hundreds at the consulate," he would say, "but the Secretary of State, Cordell Hull, and the State Department won't permit us to issue more visas."

A flight across the Pyrenees was worked out. Herta Pauli, another refugee writer, described that journey in her own words:

> Since the entire frontier zone, where the foothills of the Pyrenees meet the Mediterranean, was carefully reconnoitered, contact with the French Resistance groups were established, and through them, with Spanish anti-Fascists, to learn how to avoid French border guards and which of the Spanish could be trusted. A hike over the hills would have been exhausting at any time, but it was a blazing hot summer and the climbers were sick, demoralized and often quite old.[10]

The Feuchtwangers escaped by the same route. "We both were good mountain climbers," wrote Marta Feuchtwanger later in her own memoirs. "I was used to find my own way through foreign territory through my skiing."

They came to America and settled down in California. "My husband, Lion, never thanked Mrs. Roosevelt for what she had done for us," she also recalled. "Nor did he accept an invitation to the inauguration of the President because of an article in *Time* magazine with the allusion that Lion Feuchtwanger was a communist. Since Mrs. Roosevelt had already been attacked for her aid to refugees, Lion did not want to embarrass her."[11]

Many years later, Marta Feuchtwanger did write to Eleanor Roosevelt. "I am working on my memoirs and of course would like to describe our flight from Vichy France and how it came about. As far as I can remember that dreadful and hectic time and a discussion with the American Vice Consul, it was your instruction and the one of President Roosevelt, which made it possible for the Vice Consul to issue the American Visas which saved our lives and made it feasible to escape the Nazis." In that letter, Mrs. Feuchtwanger also asked for permission to tell that story in her forthcoming book of memoirs.[12]

"My dear Mrs. Feuchtwanger," wrote Eleanor Roosevelt in response on May 23, 1960. "Thank you for your kind letter. Of course you may write about any part I played. However, my husband was the one who was responsible for any help given. I could have done nothing except when he asked me to do it and I had his backing. I shall watch for your book with interest."[13]

The book was published in Germany under the title *Nur eine Frau* (*Only a Woman*). Later, in Berlin, a street was named in honor of Lion Feuchtwanger.

Chapter 8 ──────────────────────

The Voices of Children

"The play we saw was 'First Lady,' " wrote Jennifer W., a high school student in New York.

> It was about a lady who was poor and lived with her grandmother. Her name was Eleanor Roosevelt. When she was ten her father died. He had been drinking and fell down the stairs. Later she started working in a slum helping poor children. Left alone, she herself was poor. When she was helping the children a man came in. His name was Franklin Roosevelt. He liked her a lot. Then they got married and had five children. Then Franklin was paralyzed in his legs. Eleanor gave his speech for him for six years. Then he ran for Governor.

The play was an enormous hit. The children loved to learn about history through a musical show. They all sang along with the "hit song": "The longer I live," they sang in chorus again and again, "the more I believe, the way to receive, is to give." Another song popular with the young audience, especially the girls, was "I Refuse to Be the Woman behind the Man!"

The young people were astonished. Eleanor Roosevelt lived so long ago! Did a woman want to do her "own thing" even then. Wasn't she afraid? "To be afraid is wasting your time," they were told of Eleanor's belief. "If you keep busy helping others, you have no time to be afraid."

"Today I saw a play 'Eleanor Roosevelt,' " wrote another young student, Tina M., after seeing the show. "I enjoyed seeing such a clean play. I can't go to the movies anymore without having to see something dirty. I liked it especially when the teacher in the Boarding School explained to Eleanor Roosevelt that you have to think for yourself." Latey F. found that "it was the best play I ever saw. As a matter of fact, it was the only one I ever saw." And Bonnie T., writing from a high school in Rocky Point, New York, summed it all up by declaring, "Eleanor should have been President, because she cared about people!"[1]

John F. McHugh, the retired principal of a large comprehensive high school in Allentown, Pennsylvania, is a lifelong collector of Rooseveltiana. In 1983, he gave his students an assignment to research and write a paper on the life and works of Eleanor Roosevelt. These results prove wrong the statements of those individuals who claim that "no one cares about Eleanor Roosevelt any longer, especially the young people of today."

"An Inspiration" was the title of one student's paper. "Eleanor Roosevelt died long before I was born," he wrote. "Despite that fact, she had a profound effect upon my life and my development as a person. She was an idealist and an optimist. The former does not allow her to accept things as they are, the latter does not allow her to give up her fight for Civil Rights."

"One must remember that women in her time were not active politically," wrote Kristine W. "In her relentless crusade for Human Rights, she was indirectly one of the harbingers of the Women's movement. Eleanor Roosevelt is one of the most influential women of this century."

"Eleanor Roosevelt had love and respect for humanity that is not often seen in this world of war, hatred and suffering. Hers was a love that was extended equally to poor tenant sharecroppers or members of Royalty. She made no distinction between colors, religions or nationalities."

"Eleanor Roosevelt was a vague figure for me in American History until now," wrote yet another student. "Only by doing this research, I learned of her accomplishments. She is very much unknown to a majority of teenagers today. This should be changed. Eleanor Roosevelt was and is a role model for all of us today."

"She helped to change the values of the entire American society!"

"Eleanor Roosevelt was bold enough to resign from the Daughters of the American Revolution when they refused to allow Marian Anderson, a black singer, to perform in the Constitution Hall in Washington. She brought happiness into the lives of many Americans, if only for just a moment," was the feeling expressed by Carol T. "If beauty is in physical appearance only, then Eleanor Roosevelt was not a very beautiful woman. Yet, if personal actions and work and accomplishments are considered, then Eleanor Roosevelt was not only one of the most admired women in the world, but also one of the most beautiful women to have ever lived."

"Only a week ago, I considered Eleanor Roosevelt as merely Franklin Roosevelt's wife. Most students today do not realize the enormous quantity of her social service, the compassion for all of humanity. Instead of just attempting to survive in a world marred by competitiveness and cruelty, Mrs. Roosevelt tried to initiate social changes. Hopefully, school teachers in the future will dedicate more time to the study of her life and achievements," wrote Eli B.

"Throughout her life and her entire career, Eleanor Roosevelt fought just as many fights as Muhammed Ali did. (Maybe) and probably even more," concluded Steven I.

"Eleanor Roosevelt was the first wife of a President to hold Press conferences and travel by airplane for her husband," began Brian S. "Eleanor Roosevelt was voted the 'Most admired woman in America.' Her trips made her popular throughout the world. But her influential status took years and years of hard work and overcoming of many difficulties."

"The first thing I learned about Mrs. Roosevelt was that she was in no respect a selfish woman. She identified people in only one way: they were not black, white, Christian, or Jew. Just people, all members of the human race. When I see people saluting the flag, I often wonder whether they are saluting just a piece of decorated cloth, or if they are remembering people like Eleanor Roosevelt who made America a great nation," said Scott G.

And from Tony de Fiore: "The world today still questions Eleanor Roosevelt. Even now, many scandals follow her and her husband. But if America forgets Eleanor Roosevelt and her husband, Franklin D. Roosevelt, then America will not succeed much longer."[2]

In August 1952, a group of ten teenage Austrian exchange students came to Lakeville, Connecticut, for an "Experiment in International Living." They came from a country still occupied by the four victorious allies: England, Russia, France, and the United States.

When the Nazis marched into Austria, they had been four or five years old. Some of those students might have had memories of World War II, of frightening bombings and not much to eat. When the war ended with great defeat, they were ten or eleven years old, and now they had come to the United States of America, the country which only until seven years before had been the enemy. What did they expect? Certainly not to meet the wife of the deceased president, Eleanor Roosevelt!

And yet, there they were, sitting on a wooden porch, drinking iced cola with none other than Eleanor Roosevelt in person!

"She was so warm and friendly," remembers one of the students, Christa M., from a small village in Austria, "and she was just sitting there smiling and encouraging us to ask her about anything we wanted to know. At first we were quite shy and overwhelmed that America's First Lady took the time to be with us. But she was so natural and pleasant that we soon felt completely at ease with her."

What did Mrs. Roosevelt do with her days at the present time? one of the students wanted to know. Mrs. Roosevelt's face lit up. She liked nothing better than an opportunity to talk about the United Nations and its aims. She talked about the UN General Assembly meetings, explained what the Commission on Human Rights was seeking to accomplish, and also explained how the United States chooses, ratifies, and recompenses its delegates. Chuckling a little, she recalled one session that began at ten o'clock in the morning one day and lasted until about six o'clock in the morning the next.

"Mrs. Roosevelt impressed on us the importance of mutual understanding between nations and the greatest danger to accomplishing this was a lack of trust," Christa recalled.

"Do you think, Mrs. Roosevelt, that the United States will get tired of helping Europe when the money they send is misused in some countries?" another student wanted to know.

"In every big operation there is always waste but in most countries the funds have been used beneficially." She then spoke of the danger of fear both between nations and within a country. She said that fear is a by-product of the rise of dictators.

"Could you define democracy for us," asked another one of the students from Austria.

For a long while, Mrs. Roosevelt pondered. "Democracy is hard to define," she said then. "It is an idea you have to live with, grow up with, learn in the beginning within the family. Perhaps the best definition would be that the ideal democracy is the system of government in which every individual accepts personal responsibility with courage to think things out for himself and self-discipline."

"Isn't it true that the democracy of America would not work everywhere?" a young Austrian now asked.

"Of course!" Mrs. Roosevelt replied. "Each nation must discover its own brand of democracy. What would work for Austria would not apply in India. But there are common factors in all democracies. In all of them you will find more freedom and more personal responsibility."[3]

Upon returning home to Austria, those ten young students had the opportunity to put into action what they had learned from Mrs. Roosevelt, for in October 1955, the Vienna State Treaty was signed and Austria once more became an independent country.

"Mrs. Eleanor Roosevelt, wife of the President of the United States, yesterday paid a visit to Choate," reported the *Choate News*, in Wallingford, Connecticut, on May 11, 1940.

After having lunch in the dining hall, Mrs. Roosevelt addressed the entire student body and faculty in the private school's chapel. "We live in a democracy, which we have taken too much for granted," she told her young audience. "Every democracy in the world is fighting for its existence today, yet too often Americans act without knowing what they are acting on. Learn first what conditions exist in your own country today, and what problems have to be faced. The duties of citizenship demand that every citizen of a democracy knows not merely his own state, but his entire nation."

Then Mrs. Roosevelt invited the students to ask her questions on topics about which they wanted to know and "about which you think I might know something."

One of the questions posed was about migratory camps. Mrs. Roosevelt replied that she had recently observed the camps and was therefore able to describe them in detail. She compared the privately owned camps to those established by the government. In the latter, Mrs. Roosevelt explained, there are educational and recreational provisions made for the children of workers.

Mrs. Roosevelt then told about the previous year's visit of the king and queen of England. During his stay, the king expressed special interest in the provisions made for American youth by such organizations as the C.C.C. (Civilian Conservation Corps) and the N.Y.A. (National Youth Administration), programs which had been initiated by the Roosevelt administration. The king's interest, Mrs. Roosevelt related, was especially keen because he himself had had some experience with boys' camps and had had trouble with older boys, some of whom had never seen their fathers do a stroke of work in their lives and did not know what real work was. And so, the royal couple, accompanied by Mrs. Roosevelt, visited the C.C.C. camp.

The heat that day was overwhelming, but the king insisted on talking with the boys individually, asking them about their problems and about what the camp could do to help them. Because of the intense heat, the king was asked whether he would rather decline seeing the rest of the camp. "If the boys expect us to do it," the king replied, "we will certainly do it."

"I wonder how many of us discipline ourselves in just that way," Mrs. Roosevelt told her audience at Choate.

It is so easy to be lazy and to say that politics is a 'dirty game.' It *is* a dirty game, but when a politician is tempted to keep his job instead of doing what is right, he won't remain in office very long. In the end, it is better to do the thing that is right.

We talk a great deal about our rights, the right to say what we want to say, the right to write what we want to write, and the right to gather when we want. But we say very little about preserving these rights. You may have to give something to preserve them. If you, as individuals, are not interested in what your representatives are doing, you will get very poor service and—you will deserve it.

After her speech, Mrs. Roosevelt went to the gymnasium to watch the final rehearsal of the Choate Drama Club's presentation of *The Pirates of Penzance* and then drove back to Washington with her secretary.[4]

Chapter 9 ——————————————————————

We Remember
Mrs. Roosevelt

LADY BIRD JOHNSON

"One of my most vivid memories of Mrs. Roosevelt was one day I saw her in action," wrote Mrs. Lyndon B. Johnson.

> Lyndon was then serving in the House of Representatives, and she invited a group of congressional wives to walk with her through the slums near the Capitol. Striding along, she led us through pot-holed streets, staring children. With her as our guide, we saw another face of America which I have never forgotten.
>
> Another time, I watched her at close range when she spent two hours as guest of honor helping our 75th Congressional Club give a benefit luncheon to buy a wheelchair for a crippled boy. Only one person was involved. Where else do you start, but with one person? She cared so very much.[1]

At a tribute for Eleanor Roosevelt held at the New York Hilton in April 1964, Mrs. Johnson spoke in depth and with feeling:

> I met Eleanor Roosevelt first in print and admired her. I met her later in person and loved her. As she did to many very young and very timid congressional wives, she extended her hand and hospitality to me . . . and Washington was warmer.
>
> All of us are familiar with people who are afraid to defend un-

popular truth. Mrs. Roosevelt never stood with this timid company. Her conscience was her counselor, and she followed its commands with unfaltering courage. She did not really understand what people meant when they praised her for taking so many risks. She would have taken the greatest risk of all if she had remained silent in the presence of wrong. She would never have risked the integrity of her soul.

A rabbi of the Jewish community in Berlin under the Hitler regime once said: "The most important thing I learned is that bigotry and hatred are not the most urgent problems. The most urgent, the most disgraceful, the most shameful, and the most tragic problem — is silence." Mrs. Roosevelt knew what those words meant. She lived their meaning every day of her life. Courage sustained by compassion was the watchword of her entire career.

Always she thought not of abstract rights, but of living wrongs. She saw an unemployed father, and so she helped him. She saw a dictator hurling the world into war, and so she worked unflinchingly for peace. She saw a neglected black child, and so she educated him. She saw the United Nations divided by the conflict of ideology and power, and so she became the prophet of the Universal Declaration of Human Rights.

I saw her last when she came to my home on February 12, 1962, the day the Commission on the Status of Women was organized under her chairmanship and her inspiration. She was seventy-eight. I have often thought how much she made those years count for her country.

Let us today earnestly resolve to build the true foundation for Eleanor Roosevelt's memory — to pluck out prejudice from our lives, to remove fear and hate where it exists, and create a world unafraid to work out its destiny in peace.

Let Eleanor Roosevelt teach us all how to turn the arts of compassion into the victory of democracy.[2]

THE MORGENTHAUS

"Slowly a friendship grew with a young couple who lived in Dutchess County, New York, not far from us, Mr. and Mrs. Henry Morgenthau, Jr.," wrote Eleanor Roosevelt in her autobiography.

They were younger and perhaps for that reason we did not at first see so much of one another. We had many interests in common in the country, and Mr. Morgenthau and my husband were thrown more and more together. Mrs. Morgenthau came eventually to work in the Women's Division of the Democratic State Committee, and she and I grew gradually to have warm affection for each other. This friendship with Elinor and Henry Morgenthau is one of the things I prize most highly.[3]

Though the president's wife does not go out informally, now and then in the spring, Elinor Morgenthau and Eleanor Roosevelt would steal away in one of their cars and stop in some little place for lunch or tea.

When Mrs. Roosevelt worked for mayor of New York Fiorello La Guardia at the Office of Civilian Defense during World War II, Elinor Morgenthau volunteered as her assistant. When Franklin Roosevelt became president, he appointed Henry Morgenthau, Jr., as chairman of the Farm Administration and, in 1934, as under secretary of the Treasury.

Henry Morgenthau had a last interview with Franklin Roosevelt in Warm Springs, Georgia, the night before FDR died. Less than a month later, on May 8, 1945, the war in Europe was over. "But in that last talk with FDR," Morgenthau recalled, "Franklin was determined not to allow any sentimental considerations to modify the conditions necessary to prevent Germany and the German people from becoming aggressive again."[4]

The friendship between Eleanor Roosevelt and Elinor Morgenthau continued to the extent that when Mrs. Morgenthau was denied membership in the Colony Club in New York because she was Jewish, Eleanor Roosevelt resigned from that club.[5]

The warm feelings of Eleanor Roosevelt extended to the Morgenthaus' two sons, Robert M., the younger, and Henry, the older.

Robert M. Morgenthau is now district attorney of the County of New York—a slim, gray-haired man with discerning eyes. I visited him in his office in downtown Manhattan in December 1989. His face softened and his eyes turned nostalgic as he recalled the days of the past:

It was around 1925. We lived at 35 West Eighty-first Street in Manhattan. I was a little boy, about six years old, and I was home sick with an ear infection. My parents were away, I believe on a trip around the world. I must have been lonely. Mrs. Roosevelt came to visit me every day in the afternoon. She sometimes just looked in on me, other times she read to me. I particularly remember her bringing me a robe which I used for several years, even after it was too small for me.

Now the district attorney smiled. "There was something else," he added as his smile deepened. "While I was a student at Amherst, I was president of the Political Union and I once asked Mrs. Roosevelt to come as a speaker. She did.

" 'Oh, I am so nervous about this speech,' Eleanor Roosevelt said when I picked her up from her hotel. 'Do you think I will be all right?'"

"She really was worried," said Robert Morgenthau and chuckled. As he did, he recollected another incident.

"My mother once went on a trip with Mrs. Roosevelt to the coal mines. When they returned my mother had to go to bed for two entire days. She was totally and completely exhausted, but Eleanor Roosevelt was just fine."

Robert Morgenthau stopped, searching his memory a little more. "Oh! You must have heard about that famous visit of the king and queen of England in 1939!" he called out. "That time when Mrs. Roosevelt arranged a picnic for them in Hyde Park and served them hot dogs. *I* was the one who grilled them on an outdoor fireplace!"[6]

"WE THE PEOPLE . . ."

"I graduated from Hunter College in New York in 1942," said Ruth S. "Because of the limited seating space, each graduate was only allowed two tickets for the ceremonies. My grandmother was very unhappy that she could not come with my parents. While walking in to the commencement hall with my fellow graduates, I stared at the dais. There, seated right next to Mrs. Roosevelt, was my grandmother! She had explained her plight to Mrs. Roosevelt, who immediately had found a seat for her on the dais."[7]

"My father worked at the Roosevelt greenhouse and gardens after the estate was turned over to the federal government," said Patsy C.

While I was in high school in the mid-1950s, I made a green paper carnation for St. Patrick's Day and wired it to a real carnation stem. That day, Eleanor Roosevelt stopped at the greenhouse, as she usually did when she brought guests to the historic site. "Dink!" she called out to my father, "I didn't think carnations grow green!"

As a kid I often used to go to Val-Kill. After the Memorial Day ceremonies, Mrs. Roosevelt usually invited us for tea. I can still see her standing at the head of the table, dishing out homemade ice cream. She asked everyone whether they wanted vanilla or chocolate. If they chose vanilla, she asked if they wanted fresh strawberries on it. But she would not offer the strawberries to someone who wanted chocolate. I soon learned to ask for vanilla if I wanted strawberries also.

"Mrs. Roosevelt's habit of reporting most of the things that happened to her in her syndicated column, 'My Day,' sometimes got people upset," Elisabeth A. recalled.

One time when Mrs. Roosevelt was getting dressed for a dinner party, the zipper on her gown got stuck. Probably thinking the incident funny, she wrote about it in her newspaper column. The zipper manufacturers got very angry.

Another time, the Roosevelts purchased a new car. On the first outing, the muffler fell off in the middle of the road. The car manufacturers were not happy when they read about it in Mrs. Roosevelt's "My Day."

"I was assistant treasurer of the American Theater at the U.S.A. Pavilion during the 1958 World's Fair in Brussels," remembered Laurian B.

One morning when I opened the box office window, I saw Mrs. Roosevelt standing there on line. She wanted to buy two tickets for that evening. I chose two of the best orchestra seats available and told her that I would put her on the press list for complimentary tickets. She would not hear of this. But I persisted and asked her for the name of her hotel so that I could send them to her. She finally conceded and gave me the name of her hotel.

Just so that I could see her once more, I took off that evening and got a seat right behind her. Two young people were sitting in Mrs. Roosevelt's seats! During the intermission, I found her all the way back on the side. She had given her seats to her niece and nephew who were traveling with her, using their seats for herself.

"In the early 1950s I traveled back and forth from Smith College by airplane," remembered Caroline M.

> I was walking down a narrow hallway to one of the gates at La Guardia which was fairly empty. Walking the opposite direction was a tall woman who looked vaguely familiar. I stared at her, for the moment not realizing who she was. The tall lady smiled at me as she passed. Only later did it dawn on me that the woman in the hallway, all by herself, was none other but the former first lady, Eleanor Roosevelt.

"Mrs. Roosevelt was supposed to speak at Bushnell Hall in Hartford, Connecticut, about the United Nations," recalled Dorothy L.

> Three thousand people were expected. But by the time Mrs. Roosevelt arrived, only about three hundred people were scattered through the vast auditorium. Mrs. Roosevelt arrived, stepped onto the stage and looked around.
> "Oh, let's all come down front and be a big family," she said with her big smile, motioning the scant audience to come forward. Then she gave her speech.
> Afterward, someone asked her if she felt disappointed when, after her taking the trouble to come to our city, only such a small crowd appeared.
> "If I can reach one person only with my message about the United Nations," said Eleanor Roosevelt, "I feel that my efforts were rewarded and my time was not wasted."

"I was a kid of the Depression," said Ruth D. "My first government job was with the National Youth Association as a secretary. Around 1936, Eleanor Roosevelt was on tour through southern Illinois. She was asked to visit the coal mines there. Though it was considered bad luck at the time for a woman to go into the mines, Mrs. Roosevelt at once descended with some miners into the shafts. When she reappeared, she had a tiny coal smudge on her cheek." A famous cartoon was later made of that incident.

"My most memorable experience of my years at Vassar College was a visit from Mrs. Roosevelt," wrote Abby C.

She came to attend a performance by the Wyltwick boys, from that institution for youngsters between eight and twelve who had been in trouble with the law. Mrs. Roosevelt made it quite clear that the only purpose of her visit was to see those boys. They had come with their director, Dr. Ernst Papanek, a man with a kindly face and a heavy Viennese accent. Those boys who had so little in life seemed transformed by her presence. They flocked around her, wanted to touch her and be touched by her.

"We decided to have a ball and to invite Mrs. Roosevelt as the Queen of the Ball," wrote Don Marchese of Hopewell Junction, New York.

Marchese was the first American Field Service student to go abroad under the auspices of the Arlington High School exchange program. He went to Italy, had a great time, and when he returned, the AFS had to raise fifteen hundred dollars to send a new student overseas. They sold one-dollar tickets to a ball. Mrs. Roosevelt sent her dollar and invited Don and his mother for tea to hear more about the project. She assured them that she would do anything to foster peace and goodwill internationally, even being queen of the ball.

On the given date, Mrs. Roosevelt was escorted to a throne in the school's gym, at the center of which was a twelve-foot globe of the world. It was explained that she was the only person qualified to be queen at this event whose theme was: "Walk together, talk together, o ye people of the earth. Then and only then shall ye have peace."[8]

"At the beginning of the Spanish Civil War in the 1930's, a young Adlai Stevenson was one of the speakers at a rally in Chicago, at Orchestra Hall. Eleanor Roosevelt also spoke. After the speeches a dance program followed. The speakers were seated at the front of the stage in large, heavily carved wooden chairs," said Arline N. from Chicago. "Mrs. Roosevelt got up and started to carry her large, heavy chair to the back of the stage area. Some man quickly took it from her, but the audience gave her a big hand."

"My cousin's brother-in-law had been a student activist before World War II, then was in active service and was killed early in the war," reported that same lady.

Shortly afterward, Mrs. R. was in Chicago and went to the family's home to pay a condolence call.

When I graduated from a private teacher's college after much

financial struggle, I was not able to get a job. Many school super-
intendents would not even talk to me because I was Jewish. I was
devastated and wrote Mrs. Roosevelt about this. She replied that
indeed there was prejudice and bigotry in this country, but with
ability and perseverance I would succeed. Her words gave me
courage to go on.

"Because of a thunderstorm, Eleanor Roosevelt's plane was to land at
the airport in Lancaster, Pennsylvania," remembered Arlene W.

In 1938, there were not many planes there and my parents drove
to the airport for entertainment. They were standing there with a
baby — me — in their arms, gaping as Mrs. Roosevelt walked to her
car. She stopped for a moment, looked at me and said, "My, what
a pretty baby!"

My parents were plain, simple country folks, and this was one
of the thrills of their lives which they still remember. Just a small
gesture of kindness.

"During the 1930s and the many presidential terms of Franklin D.
Roosevelt," recalled Mr. Philip S.,

Eleanor Roosevelt was a frequent shopper at Arnold Constable,
the department store at Fifth Avenue and Fortieth Street. She ob-
tained her four inaugural gowns there. I was handling the store's
public relations, and it was my job to see to it that the newspapers
and wire services got the information.

Mrs. Roosevelt had begun shopping at the store while she was
still a young girl and her family lived nearby. Even while Mrs.
Roosevelt was First Lady, she would come strolling down the avenue, with no FBI agents in sight. Mr. Lieberman, the last owner
of the store, had a special bell signal on the desk of his third-floor
office that announced the arrival of the first lady. He then would
come down immediately to greet her and to help her personally.
Mrs. Roosevelt had a definite idea of what she wanted. Of course
she would be recognized, but always accepted stares with a smile
and gave autographs graciously. She always did her Christmas
shopping well before Thanksgiving.

One time I was flying from New York to Washington and discovered that Eleanor Roosevelt was seated right behind me. The seat next to her was vacant. She had no objections when I asked to sit next to her for a while.

I introduced myself and told her that I was of Dutch ancestry. In fact, I said, one of my grandfather's three wives was named Leila Roosevelt, and my ancestors were among the Dutch who settled in and around Albany.

"As you probably know," Mrs. Roosevelt replied, "while Franklin came from the Albany Roosevelts, my branch of the family is from Long Island and New York City, the Theodore Roosevelts. Anyhow," she added with her famous smile, "we could well be distant cousins."

On our arrival in Washington, Mrs. Roosevelt alighted with all the other passengers and, as far as I could see, was not met by any administration official or security guard. She waved goodbye and briskly stepped out of sight.

"Through the *Reader's Digest,* Mrs. Roosevelt was invited to give a speech at our local high school in Pleasantville, N.Y.," wrote Mrs. Mac-Allister. Because of heavy floodings, Mrs. Roosevelt had to take the train not to Pleasantville, but to North White Plains. After her speech, the MacAllisters found out that no provisions had been made to take Mrs. Roosevelt back to the station and offered to drive her there. She immediately accepted. "We had an old, beat-up Buick convertible," Mrs. MacAllister remembered, "and I insisted that our ten-year-old daughter sit in the back seat with me."

Mrs. Roosevelt told us that she had left Minneapolis at midnight, had had guests for breakfast and other guests for lunch, had come to Pleasantville by train to give her speech and stay throughout the following reception, and now was invited for dinner in New York. When we got to the train station, we were told that the train was delayed. When she finally left, Mrs. Roosevelt asked me if I could telephone her home in New York, to tell them that she would be twenty minutes late.

My daughter Leslie, who is now 37 years old, still remembers the warm and friendly face of Mrs. Roosevelt. But most of all, she said, she remembers Eleanor Roosevelt's voice. It was warm and personal. The voice of someone who was really listening to you, someone who really cared about what you said.[9]

"In September of 1940, I came as a freshman to Vassar College," said Nancy F. from Oklahoma.

A Republican by background, I was imbued with the conviction that Roosevelt was a devil, his wife a fiend, and their dog, Fala, a devouring snake. To my knowledge, I had never even talked to a Democrat.

In November of that year, Mrs. Roosevelt arrived at our college, turning to her Hyde Park neighbors, asking us girls — we did not think of ourselves as "women" then — to write a pamphlet to help our male counterparts adjust to their new lives in military boot camp. Fifteen or so of us met with the first lady in a prim, Victorian parlor for a first meeting. Prepared to snicker at her plain clothes, we at once were drawn in by her concern for the boys we were dating and who now were being drafted into the war. Mrs. Roosevelt's voice was gentle, but she knew exactly what it was that she wanted us to do. The Republican voice of my parents receded; the "fiend" turned into an idol. I at once volunteered to help in any way I could. We formed a committee and worked hard.

Mrs. Roosevelt came over for another afternoon tea, and we presented our program. She offered some changes, guided us quietly to reconcile viewpoints and reach new grounds. Mrs. Roosevelt made us feel equal and comfortable with her, and her involvement with us made us feel six feet tall. She radiated an excitement which I learned was the result of dedicated work. Only too soon, the project was completed, the brochure printed and distributed.

Mrs. Roosevelt thanked each one of us separately and invited us for lunch, this time at Hyde Park. On arrival there, we were told that a few other guests would be present at lunch. They were: Queen Wilhelmina of the Netherlands, Prime Minister Mackenzie King of Canada and, oh, Franklin, the president of the United States.

" 'My Mom had lunch with Eleanor Roosevelt,' my son loves to tell people," said Charlotte K. of Hyde Park.

I did have lunch with Mrs. Roosevelt, but at that time I did not really know how lucky I was. When I was my son's age, just about seventeen, I belonged to our local archery club along with my younger brother and the kids next door. One weekend we all entered into a competition, and at the end of a three-day contest, Eleanor Roosevelt was to give a luncheon to honor the winners with a trophy.

My younger brother had beaten me in all events, and I felt terrible. No way did I want to go to that luncheon, but my mother said I had to. All I could think of was my third-place medal and that I now would have to live out my life listening to my brother's bragging about his silver trophy. Well, I did obey my mother, but sulked all the way through that lunch with Mrs. Roosevelt. Still downcast, I went to school the following day and I was a celebrity! I had had lunch with Eleanor Roosevelt! And I had goofed that opportunity by sulking. To make up for this, I began to read everything about her life. Because of Eleanor Roosevelt, I still try to help someone in need as often as possible, especially underprivileged children.

Charlotte became a nurse.

"I once was stuck with Mrs. Roosevelt in an elevator," recalled Robert S., an insurance salesman in New York.

For ten minutes! I told her that this was an incredible good fortune for me, to be there with so rare and remarkable a woman. If she were a movie star, I would ask her for an autograph, I told her.

"So why don't you ask me for an autograph?" Mrs. Roosevelt asked and did not smile. "This is the trouble with our world today. Women are only seen as movie stars."

"But, Mrs. Roosevelt," I replied, "you are different from all other women. You are brilliant!"

"Young man," Eleanor Roosevelt said calmly to that, "aren't you aware that brain has no sex?"

"But woman are weaker than men," I still argued.

"Not true," Mrs. Roosevelt replied. "Some men might have more physical strength, but women have more inner strength."

I think that I am the most uninteresting fellow in the world, and yet Mrs. Roosevelt wanted to know everything about me, as if I were equal to her.

"I thought you might be interested in the story of Eleanor Roosevelt's intervention in the Prisoner of War camps in America during World War II," wrote Anna M. McKnight, wife of Major Maxwell S. McKnight, chief of the administrative section of Prisoners of War Camp Operations at that time. The camps in question were Alva, Oklahoma; Pima, Arizona; and Huntsville, Texas.

Despite strong censorship on news from those camps, stories of Nazi atrocities, murders, and forced suicides leaked to the press. Nazis were virtually running those camps. German prisoners who were anti-Nazi were beaten and terrorized in other ways if they were just caught reading the *New York Times* or listening to the radio.

"The necessity of separating Germans from Germans was at first difficult for the American army to understand," wrote Maxwell McKnight. "It never even occurred to us." Yet, Dorothy Thompson, the famous newspaper journalist, wrote in her column about those conditions of which she had heard, and began to attack the government and the military, pointing out openly that storm troopers, in effect, were domineering the camps.

"One day I received a phone call from the White House," Major McKnight recalled. " 'Mrs. Roosevelt would like you for dinner tonight,' Mrs. Roosevelt's secretary told me."

"Major McKnight, I am so glad you are here tonight," Eleanor Roosevelt said to me right in the middle of dinner with some of the other guests and members of the Roosevelt family present. "I have been hearing the most horrible stores about all the killings that are going on in our camps with these Nazi prisoners. I was told that you would be able to tell me whether there was any truth to these stories."

"Here is the Commander-in-Chief's wife," I thought. "What do you tell her?" It was a dilemma. Well, I told her so much but not the whole truth. Mrs. Roosevelt must have recognized how difficult this was for me and somehow I understood that she wanted me to speak with my superiors about my conversation with the First Lady.

I did just that and was given permission to tell everything. A couple of days later, I received another invitation to have tea with Mrs. Roosevelt. Eleanor Roosevelt, her secretary, Malvina Thompson, and I had tea on the South Portico of the White House. This time I told her everything that happened in those camps.

"I have got to talk to Franklin," Mrs. Roosevelt said. "Right in our own backyard, to have these Nazis moved in and controlling the whole thought process! What do you think this does to us?"

Mrs. Roosevelt did speak to the president, who in turn spoke to the secretaries of War and State and several generals. The army began to screen the prisoners and separated the ardent Nazis from the anti-Nazis.[10]

"In September 1943, my brother was sent overseas with the American Army," said Martha C.

It was in the midst of World War II, and we were terribly worried. Everyone in the family wrote him letters and sent packages, yet he kept writing to us asking whether we had forgotten him. He had not received any of our mail.

I did not know anymore what to do. One day, listening to the radio, I heard Arthur Godfrey and Kate Smith, the famous singer, urging everyone to write to "our boys."

I wrote about our plight to both of them, to congressmen and senators, and also to Eleanor Roosevelt. I grew up with Mrs. Roosevelt, read her column "My Day" religiously, and felt as if the first lady was my personal friend.

Eleanor Roosevelt was the only one who replied to my letter. She advised me to take her letter to APO headquarters, which would admit me to someone in charge. I did.

My Eleanor Roosevelt letter was like a passport that opened doors for me. I found out where my brother was stationed, and our mail finally was forwarded to him.

Dr. Hans Hannau, police commissioner of Vienna before the Nazi takeover, came as a political refugee to America in the early 1940s. At that time, a friend of his, Otto Kallir, opened an art gallery, St. Etienne, on West Fifty-seventh Street in New York, and Dr. Hannau attended the opening. Present also was the first lady, Eleanor Roosevelt. Dr. Hannau was introduced to her, and while they chatted, a newspaper photographer snapped a picture of them.

Later, Dr. Hannau traveled through the United States and, as an enthusiastic photographer, took pictures along the way. When his bus passed through Baltimore, the sun was very bright and Dr. Hannau decided to get off to take some photographs. After he picked out a view he liked, Dr. Hannau went into a building to ask permission from the superintendent to go with his camera to the roof. As he spoke with a heavy Viennese accent and, after all, the country was at war, the superintendent became suspicious and told him to wait. When he returned he was accompanied by three burly policemen. Suspecting he was a Russian spy, they wanted to arrest him. Searching for his identification, Dr. Hannau dropped the newspaper photo with Mrs. Roosevelt, which he always carried with him. The policemen picked it up, gazed at it for a long while, then decided to let Dr. Hannau go.[11]

"It was back in 1951 or 1952 when I read in the local paper that Mrs. Roosevelt would be coming to Tucson to give a talk at the university," Jeraldine P. remembered.

It also said that she would be staying at the Arizona Inn. On an impulse, I bought one dozen roses. They were called "Eleanor Blue." I never saw that particular shade again. I sent them to Mrs. Roosevelt and wrote a brief note to let her know that we all loved her. Never did I expect to hear from her, but only a few days later, I received a handwritten note from Eleanor Roosevelt to thank me. I had it framed. The handwriting was shaky, hard to make out, but it said: "Appreciate—warm thanks."

Such a busy lady, yet never too busy to say "thank you."

To Jack Greenway, owner of the famed Arizona Inn, Mrs. Roosevelt was "Aunt Eleanor." His mother, Isabella, was a lifelong close friend of Eleanor Roosevelt, a bridesmaid at her wedding, and a godmother to her daughter, Anna.

"Aunt Eleanor was an incredibly disciplined person," Jack Greenway recalled.

She was at all times flawlessly punctual. Once, when she came here to give a lecture at the Jewish Community Center, she received a bouquet of flowers with a card signed by six ladies. Aunt Eleanor insisted on writing six individual thank-you notes. Another time she came with some friends from New York, strictly on a vacation. She told us that it was the first vacation of her life. Until then, "vacation" only meant to her the time when the cook took time off and Eleanor Roosevelt herself made sandwiches and pots of coffee.[12]

Mary Jeffries started the Sunday Evening Forum at the University of Arizona in Tucson in 1952. One day Eleanor Roosevelt came as a speaker on "The United Nations Today." The event was free and open to the public. The night of Mrs. Roosevelt's talk, a bitter-cold November night, the auditorium was overflowing with people. Hundreds who could not be admitted were milling outside. When Mrs. Roosevelt arrived, the door to the auditorium was opened for her. She took a look around and stopped. "First I must speak to the people out here!" she said. Seemingly oblivious of the cold, Eleanor Roosevelt first gave her talk under the stars.[13]

"I met Mrs. Roosevelt when she worked at Hull-House, a settlement house on the Lower East side of New York," said Mrs. H. who presently sells table linen at a department store in Tucson. "She always was so kind, never put on airs."

Carl B. is of German descent and during World War II, the children in school taunted him about his background. "I was a very lonely child," he remembers still. But he also remembers that, when he went shopping with his mother at the department stores in New York, they would often meet Mrs. Roosevelt at Altman's. "She would never forget to ruffle my hair and tell me she was glad to see me." He also recalls that it was Eleanor Roosevelt who insisted to President Truman that the rulings that black people had to sit at the back of a bus in the South must be stopped. Eleanor Roosevelt was the mother of America, Carl B. is convinced.

Nancy K.'s father owned the famous radio program "Twenty Questions," which was on the air from 1946 to 1955. One day Mrs. Roosevelt was invited to be a guest on the program. The question prepared for her was to guess the name of the dog of a famous president. Characteristic of Eleanor Roosevelt's self-effacing ways, it took her quite a while to realize that the name being thought of was none other but "Fala."

Alice B. was working at the Bethesda Naval Hospital in Maryland in 1943. She remembers the president coming there for treatments. "Mrs. Roosevelt was always with him, helping with the wheelchair, walking beside him, seeing to it that he was all right."

Mrs. W., at ninety, still remembers when she lived in Washington in 1940 and worked for the British Red Cross. "Oh, you are working here again today," Mrs. R. would say when she came in, looking straight at her face. "She always looked at people. She really looked and listened. She had a way of making you feel six feet tall."

Back in 1925, we used to live on Madison Avenue and Sixtieth Street, near where the Roosevelts lived. We used to meet Mrs. Roosevelt often at the neighborhood drugstore," recalled Robert S. "She would take one or the other of her boys for breakfast there, and she never failed to give us a smile and to say, 'Hello.' "

In June 1932, Solomon A. was one of the graduates of the High School of Commerce in New York City. Along with the other boys, he snickered about the tall, gawky lady who was so plain, so angular, accompanying their principal as he entered the auditorium. "Who is she?" the boys began to whisper. Someone quickly hushed them. They were told that the lady was the wife of the governor of New York, Mrs. Roosevelt. "Poor guy," the boys giggled even more when they heard that "high, silly tone of her voice." Yet unaccountably, they all soon fell silent and listened. "We applauded thunderously when she finished. Suddenly we all thought that Eleanor Roosevelt was beautiful."

David W. served with the Naval Contruction Battalion in Trinidad in 1943. He recalls all the fun comedians used to make at that time of Mrs. Roosevelt's travels. "But no one in Trinidad thought it was funny when she came and told us: 'The president wants me to tell you that he thinks you are doing a great job and he wants to thank you for all your efforts.' "

"When I traveled to Israel, I became friendly with the Reverend Gordon L. Kidd, rector of St. James's Church in Hyde Park," remembered Helen H.

He told us that it was Mrs. Roosevelt who had sent him and his wife, Claire, on that trip because she wanted them to see the country.
Back home, the Kidds invited me for dinner and also present was Mrs. Roosevelt. I helped Claire to clear the table, and because of Mrs. Roosevelt's presence, I tried to be especially ele-

gant, carrying only one plate at a time to kitchen. Not so Mrs. Roosevelt. She too helped by simply piling a whole bunch of plates right on top of each other. Later, I often had lunch with Mrs. Roosevelt at the United Nations cafeteria in New York and she always insisted on carrying her own tray.

Lee C.'s mother was the only Democrat in her family when they lived in the Midwest during the Depression. One day when Eleanor Roosevelt was expected to pass through town on a train, Lee's mother permitted him to cut school in order to see her. Mexican workers were busy on the tracks, and the train with the distinguished passenger had to wait until they were done. A bouquet of flowers was brought to them with a card thanking them for making that trip possible. Since the workers only spoke Spanish, Eleanor Roosevelt had written the note in shorthand.

Dorothy Rosenman, wife of Judge Rosenman, the woman who cried, in the Governor's Mansion in Albany awaiting the nomination of Franklin D. Roosevelt for president, remembered another evening when Eleanor Roosevelt came to New York from Albany to have dinner with the Rosenmans at their apartment on Central Park West.

They lived in one of those old apartment houses with large, elegant rooms, high ceilings, and very thick walls. In one of those walls, lived a mouse. No matter how hard they tried, the Rosenmans could not get rid of it. The mouse outsmarted their every attempt.

After dinner with Mrs. Roosevelt, they were all sitting in the living room chatting when the mouse appeared. Dorothy and her husband exchanged mortified glances. The mouse remained sitting there right in the middle of the carpet, getting up on its haunches and looking at them. Dorothy desperately tried to divert her distinguished guest to look in another direction. It was to no avail.

"Why, Dorothy!" Eleanor called out before long in her high-pitched voice. "Look! Over there! You have a mouse!" She chuckled while she pointed to it.[14]

"Mrs. Roosevelt would like to invite you to tea day after tomorrow at three-thirty," Henry Viscardi, Jr., was informed by Mrs. Roosevelt's secretary over the phone sometime during World War II. Mrs. Roosevelt often invited people who interested her to tea, but this invitation was special. Henry Viscardi was a man born without legs.

Born on May 10, 1912, the second child and only son of an immigrant

Italian barber and his wife, the baby's short thighs ended in two small stumps. After extensive hospital treatments over the next two years, Henry was taken home and was given a little wagon on which he pushed himself around.

One day a young doctor who just had opened his office in the neighborhood, Robert Yanover, stopped him on the street. The two became friends, and the doctor helped Henry to get more treatments. By the time he was four, his short limbs were reasonably straight, and he got a pair of leather orthopedic boots in which he could walk and run. Henry finished high school and went on to Fordham University. He got a job in the treasurer's office and also worked as a busboy in the freshmen dining room. When his father died, in spite of his handicap, Henry partially supported the family, but after several years, his stumps were "burned out."

Dr. Yanover took Henry to a designer of prosthetic appliances. After many months and agonizing work, Henry's aluminum legs were completed. At the age of twenty-five, Henry finally was a man, five feet eight inches tall. Slowly, painfully, first with crutches, and finally without, Henry began to walk. He burned his old clothes, his sister taught him how to dance, he began going out with girls, and he bought a boat to go sailing on the Sound.

December 7, 1941. The Japanese Air Force and Navy attacked Pearl Harbor. Henry Viscardi offered his services to his country. "What can you do?" the authorities asked, their faces expressing their doubt about a man without legs. "There is something I can do better than anyone else," Henry replied. "I can teach men who lose their legs how to walk again." The authorities stalled, but Henry persisted. Finally he was appointed Army Captain of Field Services and put on duty at Walter Reed Hospital in Washington. There he met Dr. Howard Rusk, who headed the Air Force's Convalescences Training Division that worked with amputees. Henry was dismayed by the hospital's poor equipment to meet the great demand of war veterans who were amputees. The legs the patients got after too-long periods of time were so poorly constructed that they often broke the first time they were used. He reported these findings to Dr. Howard Rusk. He told him that the prosthetic shop was tiny and totally inadequate. The limb maker wanted to build a cart for a man who needed legs.

One day Henry began teaching a Major Robinson how to walk. The major, who had been a fighter pilot, on another day cut short his lesson because he was invited for dinner at the White House. It was soon after that Henry received the phone call from Mrs. Roosevelt's secretary.

"I hear you are doing some wonderful work," Eleanor Roosevelt said, with a wide smile and outstretched hands. "Are you having difficulties putting your program over?"

Before he realized what he was doing, Henry told her the complete story of his life, including problems at the hospital. Eleanor Roosevelt listened to him for an entire hour.

"I think perhaps I can help you," she said then. The wheels started to turn.

Three weeks later, Henry Viscardi was called to tell his story to the chief of the Air Force. Pressure for improved conditions for pilots started at once. Parents from all over the country were writing to their congressmen and complaining about the amputee program.

Congress began to move. Walter Reed Hospital expanded the shop for prosthetic appliances to three times its former size; they hired a large staff of physical therapists; a new amputation center was put in operation in Michigan. The National Research Council set up a committee to work on the improvement of artificial limbs, which was the beginning of a program that today provides disabled soldiers with the finest prosthetic appliances the world has ever known. And Eleanor Roosevelt became a lifelong friend to Henry Viscardi.

"Mrs. Roosevelt was my first client of importance," remembered W. Colston Leigh.

In 1929, the year of the stock market crash in America and the beginning of the Great Depression, Leigh started what was to become the noted Leigh Lecture Bureau. At that time he was twenty-eight years old, earned about twenty-five dollars a week, and was looking for clients. He was desperately looking for clients.

Through a mutual acquaintance, Eleanor Roosevelt heard about the young man's plight and invited him to Val-Kill. She informed him that she wanted him to become her booking agent for lectures—or rather for the informal talks Mrs. Roosevelt used to give. From that time in 1929 until almost the day she died, he booked her lectures for her.

A large, signed, framed photograph in Leigh's possession shows Eleanor Roosevelt looking tall and regal in a gown with a train. It was taken at the White House on the occasion of Franklin D. Roosevelt's birthday ball. Leigh had been invited to the event, and he had to buy his first tails and white tie.

In a room at the White House, as he got dressed for the ball, he simply did not know what to do with his tie. Just as he was in the midst of his despair, there was a knock at the door. "Would you like me to help you with your tie, Colston?" Mrs. Roosevelt asked. "I always do it for Franklin."

"Mrs. Roosevelt never lectured while a congressman or a senator was running for office," Leigh recalled.

Her lectures could never be a political campaign for someone while her husband was president. Usually, while Congress was in session, Mrs. Roosevelt did not lecture at all. She also did not lecture in foreign countries because she felt it would look like propaganda. Her lectures always were just about people being people. Later on, of course, she used to talk mainly about the United Nations and human rights. She also lectured at women's clubs, many Jewish groups like the UJA, and of course she was a very popular speaker at colleges and universities. But Mrs. Roosevelt never talked to business groups, and when she spoke for the Democratic Party she never accepted a fee.

I could easily have gotten as much as $5,000 for a lecture given by Mrs. Roosevelt, perhaps even more, but she never permitted me to charge more than fifteen hundred dollars. Mrs. Roosevelt felt that a high fee would deprive some people from hearing what she wanted them to know about the UN and other humanitarian matters. Anyway, she kept only enough money to cover her expenses from those fees. The rest always went to her favorite charities, such as the Wiltwyck School for Boys, the UJA, all those things she believed in.[15]

Mr. Leigh did not think that the president liked him. He had a little Scottish terrier, much like Fala. Fala seemed to recognize the scent and would trot over to Leigh to sniff his legs. "Now Fala was the president's dog," Mr. Leigh said and laughed. "And FDR let me know that by the way he glared at me.

"I saw Mrs. Roosevelt just about a month before she passed away on November 7, 1962," W. Colston Leigh ended his story. "She thought it would be safe to book a lecture in about a month or so. She was confident that she would get better."[16]

In February 1953, the class of 1947 was having its yearly get-together at the Harvard Club of New York City. The task of finding an appropriate speaker for the dinner fell to Donald Cummings. Past speakers had been figures from the world of sports, in which Cummings was not particularly interested. On a sudden inspiration, he invited Eleanor Roosevelt to be speaker for the evening.

"Eleanor Roosevelt?" asked one of his classmates, a staunch Republican. But everyone else was enthusiastic. At first, Cummings was afraid that she would decline. The dinner was a small event, and Mrs. Roosevelt was, as everyone knew, so very busy. Yet, she accepted. The response from Cummings's classmates was overwhelming: Reservations came pouring in.

On the morning of the dinner, Cummings got a phone call from Mrs. Roosevelt's secretary. Since her former secretary, "Tommy," Malvina Thompson, who had been with her for thirty years, was seriously ill (she died that year on April 12), Mrs. Roosevelt just possibly would not be able to attend. Cummings was dismayed: The event was fully booked and he had no replacement. In the afternoon, however, he got another phone call: Mrs. Roosevelt would be able to appear as arranged.

At that time, the Harvard Club had a strict rule that women could enter those hallowed premises only when invited by a male escort—and, at that, only by a side door and a rather steep staircase leading up to a ladies' lounge and the ladies' dining room. Cummings appealed to the board to make an exception for Eleanor Roosevelt: She was, after all, the former first lady and had resided at the White House for twelve years. His appeal was rejected.

Picking Mrs. Roosevelt up at the Park Sheraton Hotel, where she resided at that time, he embarrassedly explained his predicament. "I understand," Mrs. Roosevelt said. And that was the last mention of that situation.

She entered the side entrance, climbed the staircase to the ladies' lounge, crossed it and entered the ladies' dining room, then followed Cummings through several back hallways and finally climbed another staircase to the Biddle Room, where the dinner took place. Eleanor Roosevelt, it would appear, would suffer any inconvenience for the opportunity to bring her message about the importance of the United Nations and the new Declaration for Human Rights to as many people as possible—especially to the young, whom she saw as the future of the country. During the talk, the audience was so silent that one could have heard a pin drop on the polished floor.

It was not until 1972 that the club finally called a vote to drop restrictions concerning women. The first vote was a rejection of the proposal, but on the second vote it passed.[17]

MAUREEN CORR

"The story and the interest continue," said Maureen Corr during a telephone conversation on November 7, 1991, the twenty-ninth anniversary of the death of Eleanor Roosevelt.

Maureen had acted as a private secretary to Eleanor Roosevelt during the last twelve years of her life. Born in Armagh, Northern Ireland, Maureen arrived in the United States when she was seventeen years old. She graduated from Hunter College and afterward took education courses at Columbia University, aiming to become a teacher. Instead of reaching that goal, she took a job as a secretary to an eye specialist at Columbia Presbyterian Medical Center. While quite happy with her work, Maureen did not find it completely satisfying. One day she decided to register with a New York employment agency. That day's decision changed Maureen's life.

The agency immediately scheduled an interview for her. While taking the elevator down, Maureen glanced at the name of the potential employer to whom she was to report. She gasped. Assistant secretary to Eleanor Roosevelt! Never would she be accepted, Maureen thought.

It was not Mrs. Roosevelt who conducted the interview but her present personal secretary, Malvina Thompson, whose assistant she would be. She was hired at once and started work on November 1, 1950, at the Park Sheraton Hotel, where Mrs. Roosevelt lived at that time. Eleanor was in South America, but a week later she appeared at the office.

"I am Eleanor Roosevelt," she said with her wide smile as she approached Maureen's desk. As if Maureen did not know who she was! Did Mrs. Roosevelt really believe that people did not know her?

The office was a very busy one, and at first Maureen saw little of "Mrs. R.," as the staff referred to her. Then, at the end of 1951, Malvina Thompson, who was with Mrs. R. in Paris for the United Nations Human Rights Commission, became ill. Maureen was asked to accompany Mrs. R. to the General Assembly meeting in Paris after the Christmas recess. Maureen was stunned. She was going to go to Paris? With Mrs. R.? It was quite incredible!

Mrs. Roosevelt and Maureen took the midnight flight from Idlewild Airport on December 31, 1951. After shaking hands and greeting several people on board, Mrs. R. wrapped herself in a large blanket and settled down in the two seats provided for her for the overnight flight. Maureen was seated across the isle. Since it was New Year's Eve, everyone was in high spirits and toasted the New Year with champagne, but Mrs. Roosevelt slept soundly throughout the journey.

Unaccustomed to champagne, Maureen got a little worried as she recalled her first trip back to Ireland when the change in time and excitement left her sleepless for several nights afterward. Feeling that she simply could not afford a recurrence of that experience on this vital trip for her, she took a sleeping pill. The combination of the pill and the champagne was disastrous. When the plane landed in Paris the next day Maureen was completely exhausted. Not so, Mrs. R. Having slept well throughout the night, she was full of energy and raring to go.

They checked into the Hotel de Crillon and Maureen was shown to a cosy room with a big bed with a golden satin eiderdown quilt. How inviting it looked! However, Mrs. R. had other plans instead of resting. She immediately scheduled a conference with some members of the U.S. mission, lunch with her granddaughter, Sistie, and family, then a drive through the Bois de Boulogne, followed by afternoon tea, and so on.

Maureen became drowsier and drowsier but tried to keep in step. At long last, when everything was attended to and Maureen thought she would finally be able to slide under that delicious eiderdown, Mrs. R. remembered that they still had to work on her column, "My Day." Somehow Maureen muddled through until Mrs. R. announced, "This will be all for today, though I still have some personal letters to write."

Maureen crept to her room. She thought that Mrs. R. must have found her a complete failure. But before she even began to undress there was a light tap on her door. Mrs. R. came into Maureen's room looking fresh and glowing in her blue dressing gown.

"It has been a very long day, Maureen, and you must be tired," she said with her warm smile. "But everything is going to be all right. I think we are going to manage beautifully." Then, giving Maureen a light kiss on the cheek, she bade her a good night.

Maureen still recalls how she felt after this so unexpected and so gracious gesture. Had Mrs. R. asked her to work around the clock, she would have gladly done so.

That first trip to Paris was the start of a round-the-world journey. Many other trips followed in the twelve marvelous years Maureen spent in Mrs. R.'s employment—years that still keep bringing excitement and new interests into her life. Hardly a day goes by without a phone call from someone asking for information about Mrs. Roosevelt or from someone she met on her world trips, or an invitation to some Hyde Park or Washington function.[18] Indeed the story is not over—not for Maureen, not for the many, many people the world over who knew and loved Eleanor Roosevelt, not for the innumerable people whom she helped.

No, the story is not over by a long shot, it will continue without end, for Eleanor Roosevelt is an indelible part of the very best of our history.

Bearing out Maureen's proof that the story is not over is the project for an Eleanor Roosevelt Monument to be erected in 1994 in Riverside Park in New York.

In 1986, Herbert Zohn, a retired art dealer, had a dream. Living on Riverside Drive, he deplored the condition of a patch of ground at the corner of Riverside Park and Seventy-second Street, leading to the Henry Hudson Parkway. There, in the middle of some sad-looking plants, stood a pedestal without a monument. Passing that orphaned pedestal one day, Zohn, a lifelong admirer of Eleanor Roosevelt, had an abrupt vision of a sculpture of Mrs. Roosevelt occupying that abandoned spot.

It took many years and endless efforts to turn that dream into reality. Red tape and more red tape had to be dealt with, but a great many people helped. An Eleanor Roosevelt Monument Fund was created, and an honorary committee with many distinguished names was formed. Twelve artists were invited to submit designs, and Boston-based sculptor Penelope Jencks was selected. Her plan shows an eight-foot figure leaning on a natural rock, resting her chin in one hand while gazing into the distance. In May 1991, the design was approved by the Landmarks Preservation Commission, and now, Herbert Zohn's dream will be realized.

The Eleanor Roosevelt Monument will be the very first public statue of a woman who actually lived, outside of Joan of Arc, in New York City.[19]

Chapter 10 _____

Farewell to
Eleanor Roosevelt

ST. JAMES CHURCH, HYDE PARK

The Reverend Gordon L. Kidd served as a navy chaplain during World War II. After the war, he came directly to Hyde Park to serve at St. James, which was built in 1844. The Episcopal church was visited regularly through the years by the Roosevelt family, including Eleanor.

"She loved people," remembered Reverend Kidd, "and she wanted to talk to them all the time to learn their story. 'Everybody has a story,' she used to say. And she was always very patient, signing cards and autographing books." He continued,

Mrs. Roosevelt also often brought famous foreign visitors to the church, such as Haile Selassie, the emperor of Ethiopia, and Queen Juliana of the Netherlands. The only people she did not bring were Nikita Khrushchev and his wife, Nina. Mrs. Roosevelt said that Russians did not like any connection with religion. But everyone else she wanted me and my wife, Claire, to meet.

The Roosevelt pew in the church is the third one from the front on the left, and it stands out. Mrs. Roosevelt was quite tall, and of course, when she stood up, everyone could see her.

On the last two Sundays when she came to church she did not rise. All during the service, Mrs. Roosevelt remained seated. Afterward she apologized to me. At long last she admitted that she was too tired. Yet death held no fear for Eleanor Roosevelt, though she did not believe in a life after death.[1]

Eleanor Roosevelt wished to give her body—any part of it, but especially her eyes—to any medical school or individual who could use them. In the end, this wish could not be fulfilled. Eleanor Roosevelt had been too ill.

THE FUNERAL

November 7, 1962, was a sad, gray day. Eleanor Roosevelt had died. The funeral services would take place at St. James in Hyde Park, on November 10. Her final resting place was to be in the Rose Garden of the mansion, beside her husband with the very small one of their dog just behind.

A great many people came to Hyde Park to attend the funeral, and the town itself was closed down. They came from all parts of the country, but St. James could not accommodate them. Secret Service men were everywhere.

President John F. Kennedy had arrived with his wife from Washington. Vice President Johnson was also attending, as were former presidents Eisenhower and Truman. Herbert Hoover had sent a message; if he had not been too ill, he would have come too. Many senators were present, even several Republicans, such as Governor Rockefeller of New York.

Mrs. Roosevelt had made it known that she did not want any flowers on her casket, just fir boughs.

Danny Kaye was standing at the grave site as the casket was lowered, and tears were streaming down his face. And then it was over.

"Well, now we are really on our own," a man was overheard murmuring as he departed. "Like so many orphans."[2]

DEDICATION OF THE ELEANOR ROOSEVELT WING AT THE FDR LIBRARY, HYDE PARK

May 3, 1972, is a gray day with the clouds hanging heavily over New York City. Three chartered buses are standing before the building on West Fifty-seventh Street that houses the Eleanor Roosevelt Foundation. People are arriving carrying umbrellas: old people, young people, strangers who smile at each other. It is nearly ten years since Eleanor Roosevelt died. "I was very close to Mrs. Roosevelt," says a tall man with a Southern drawl. "I met her forty years ago and she sort of adopted me. I flew in this morning from Arkansas, just for this ceremony." "I came in from Georgia," volunteers another man. "I am the director of the 'Little White House' in Warm Springs. We knew Mrs. Roosevelt well."

People keep coming, and a lady with a pleasant smile checks the names on her list. One bus fills up and promptly at nine o'clock leaves the city behind.

The passengers are pleasantly quiet as the bus drives up along the Hudson River. Some strike up muted conversations. "I met her on an airplane to London once." "She invited me for lunch at Val-Kill." "I had tea with her in her apartment on Washington Square."

Some two hours later, a white sign appears at the side of the road. On it is the silhouette of a man with glasses and an up-tilted cigarette holder. Franklin D. Roosevelt. "Welcome to Hyde Park," it says.

State troopers direct the traffic before the Roosevelt estate. It is raining now, and people open their umbrellas as they walk to the FDR Library.

A group of people is gathered before the new wing. Two workmen place the cornerstone into the wall. "In memory of Eleanor Roosevelt," it says. Some faces in front of the group look very familiar, almost as if Franklin and Eleanor were present themselves. They belong to their daughter and four sons: Anna, sixty-six; James, sixty-five; Elliot, sixty-two; Franklin, Jr., fifty-eight; and John, fifty-six. And there is a cluster of many Roosevelt grandchildren and great-grandchildren.

The cornerstone is plastered into place, lightbulbs flash, cameras click, but it is still a half hour before the ceremony.

The guests wander off, some to the gravesite of Franklin and Eleanor in the Rose Garden, where the white marble headstone with its clean lines glows in the gray fog. Fresh spring flowers are on the graves, some even on the very small one of Fala, the most famous black Scottish terrier in history.

The rain becomes heavier, so guests saunter toward the Roosevelt home. Many of the people entering are famous from newspapers and television. Among them are labor leader David Dubinsky and Joseph Lash, who had just received the Pulitzer Prize for his momentous biography, *Eleanor and Franklin*. "I was Mrs. Roosevelt's secretary," a young woman with a trace of Irish in her voice introduces herself. "I was her last maid," says another woman who speaks with an Austrian accent.

The troopers explain the interior of the house. They point out the massive oak wardrobe in the main hall and the eighteenth-century grandfather clock that James and Sara Roosevelt purchased in the Netherlands in 1881. They show the snuggery, Sara's writing and sitting room, and the living room with its two large fireplaces and the two chairs Franklin Roosevelt received while he was governor of New York—one for each term. Upstairs are the room where Franklin was born and the large room overlooking the Hudson River where he slept until his death.

It is almost three o'clock, and the ceremony is about to begin. The six hundred visitors walk toward the red-striped tent which has been put up in front of the library. The Reverend Gordon L. Kidd, rector emeritus of St. James Church, gives the invocation. He prays that we can go on to live in liberty.

The chairman of the Executive Committee of the Eleanor Roosevelt Foundation welcomes the guests, then he dedicates the new wing. Dr. James B. Rhoads, archivist of the United States, accepts it on behalf of the United States Government. The next speaker is Anna Roosevelt Halstead.

"This is indeed the time of women's liberation," she says with a smile which reminds one of her mother. "I never thought I would see the day when my four brothers would agree to let me be the speaker for the family." She goes on to tell the gathering about the ways of her parents. "We have learned to outgrow our childish notion that our parents belong to us," she says with earnest warmth. "Our father and mother belonged to the world."

The great singer Marian Anderson speaks next. "Why are so many of us here today?" she asks, also giving the answer, "because of love. Love for Eleanor Roosevelt and her love for mankind."

The secretary general of the United Nations speaks of Mrs. Roosevelt's role in the United Nations. Then Governor Rockefeller, who had trouble flying in, rushes to the microphone with greetings from the president.

Now everyone hurries through the rain to the library's new wing, which houses the papers of Eleanor Roosevelt, all three million pages. Two wings were actually added to the original building and dedicated in her honor: one houses enlarged research facilities; the other contains an exhibit gallery devoted to Mrs. Roosevelt's life and career and an auditorium where part of the president's naval collection is displayed. Films and slides on the Roosevelt era may be shown there, and meetings, lectures, and seminars held.

The visitors wander around, admiring the bright new rooms. The pictures on the walls bring back memories to many, as one can hear from snatches of conversations. Here is Mrs. Roosevelt in her Red Cross uniform; there is a photograph of her as a very young girl. Gifts from heads of state the world over are displayed, as are pictures of Eleanor with her babies and her mother-in-law. There are the clothes she used to wear: an inauguration gown, a fur piece she was fond of.

Many of the visitors stop for a long while before a glass case that displays Eleanor Roosevelt's very old, very well-worn red wallet. Its contents are spread out: her driver's license, a card willing her eyes to the Eye Bank, a scrap of paper with Eleanor Roosevelt's handwriting: "A day in which you have not done a kindness is a day lost."

People are quiet on the bus driving back to the city. The air is chilly and damp, yet these strangers seem linked together by a bond of warmth. Lingering in their minds might still be the vision of the flame-shaped crystal at the entrance to the new exhibition hall. Two hands etched in the glass stretch upward, and upon the base is the famous quotation from Adlai Stevenson's eulogy to Eleanor Roosevelt:

> She would rather light a candle than curse the darkness, and her glow has warmed the world.

Chronology

THE EARLY YEARS

1884 (Oct. 11)	Anna Eleanor Roosevelt born to Anna (Hall) and Elliott Roosevelt in New York City at 11 West 37th Street.
1892 (Dec. 7)	Mother died. Eleanor and brothers (Hall and Elliott) sent to live with Grandmother Hall. Elliott died several months later.
1894 (Aug. 14)	Father died.
1899–1902	Attended Mlle Souvestre's school, Allenswood, in South Fields, England.
1902	Volunteer for Junior League. Taught calisthenics and dancing at the Rivington Street Settlement House. Worked with Consumer's League, investigating working conditions in garment factories and department stores.
1905 (Mar. 17)	Married Franklin Delano Roosevelt.
1906 (May 3)	Anna Eleanor born.
1907 (Dec. 23)	James born.
1909 (Mar. 18)	First Franklin D. Roosevelt, Jr., born. Died Nov. 8, 1909.
1910 (Sep. 23)	Elliott born.
1914 (Aug. 17)	Franklin D. Roosevelt, Jr., born.
1916 (Mar. 13)	John born.
1917	Joined Red Cross canteen. Involved in organizing Navy Red Cross. Instrumental in initiating move to improve con-

	ditions at St. Elizabeth's Hospital, Washington, D.C. Helped start occupational therapy work program for servicemen. Persuaded Red Cross to build recreation rooms for servicemen.
1920	Joined board of League of Women Voters. Responsible for reports on national legislation of interest to league.
1922	Joined Women's Trade Union League. Met Marion Dickerman and Nancy Cook—start of close friendship which lasted until 1938. Became finance chairman of women's division of the State Democratic Committee. Did organizational work and printed newsletter for them.
1924	In charge of committee that presented to the Resolution Committee planks of interest to women of the National Democratic Convention. Helped organize state campaigns. Idea of building cottage at Val-Kill conceived.
1926	Val-Kill cottage completed.
1927	Val-Kill Industries, a humanitarian experiment to stem flow of youth from rural to urban areas by providing employment during the slack farm season, started.
1928	Involved in organizing support among women in the presidential campaign for Al Smith.

THE YEARS AS FIRST LADY

1933	Sponsored the Arthurdale Project, an experiment in Reedsville, West Virginia: Federal government would resettle families, provide housing, and try to attract new industry to train and employ the miners.
1936	Began to write "My Day," a daily column in the form of a diary of her days at the White House. Column continued until 1962. In May Val-Kill Industries dissolved. Shortly thereafter, had factory building converted into an apartment for herself and her secretary, Malvina Thompson.
1941–42	Worked in Office of Civilian Defense in conjunction with Mayor La Guardia.
1942	Trip to England to observe role of British women in war effort.
1943–44	Trips to Pacific and Caribbean to visit military and Red Cross installations.
1945 (Apr. 12)	FDR died in Warm Springs, Georgia.

THE YEARS ALONE

1946 (Apr. 12)	Turns Springwood (FDR's home) over to federal government. Val-Kill becomes permanent home.
1946	Member of the United States delegation to the organizational meeting of the UN General Assembly. Chairman of Commission on Human Rights.
1946–52	Appointed U.S. delegate to the United Nations General Assembly.
1950–62	Hosted TV talk show later entitled "Prospects of Mankind."
1952–62	Traveled to countries including India, Lebanon, Syria, Jordan, Pakistan, Turkey, Greece, Yugoslavia, Japan, Morocco, Belgium, and the U.S.S.R. to study their standards of living and customs.
1953	Began work for the American Association for the United Nations. Malvina Thompson died.
1955	Delegate to the World Federation of United Nations Associations.
1956	Actively campaigned for Adlai Stevenson for president.
1959	Launched new career as visiting lecturer at Brandeis University.
1960	Involved in the presidential campaigns, first of Stevenson, then of John F. Kennedy.
1961	Member of the U.S. Delegation to the Special Session of the General Assembly. Served on the Advisory Council of the Peace Corps. Presided over the commission on the Status of Women.
1962 (Nov. 7)	Died in New York at the age of 78. Buried next to husband in Rose Garden in Hyde Park on Nov. 10.
1972 (May 3)	The Eleanor Roosevelt Gallery and wing in the FDR Library in Hyde Park dedicated.
1977 (May 26)	Congress authorized establishment of Eleanor Roosevelt National Historic Site at Val-Kill.

───────────────────────────

Quotations of
Eleanor Roosevelt

The only way to make friends is to be friendly. It is what you give of yourself that makes friends for you.

Ladies' Home Journal, April 1942

Happiness is not a goal, it is a by-product.

You Learn by Living, p. 95

Life was meant to be lived and curiosity must be kept alive. One must never, for whatever reason, turn his back on life.

Autobiography of Eleanor Roosevelt, p. 19

There is a wonderful word, why?, that children use. All children. When they stop using it, the reason, too often is that no one bothered to answer them.

You Learn by Living, p. 10

I have never wanted to be a man. I have often wanted to be more effective as a woman, but I never felt that trousers would do the trick!

Ladies' Home Journal, October 1941

No one can make you feel inferior without your consent.

This Is My Story

You gain strength, courage and confidence by every experience in which you really stop to look fear in the face. You are able to say to yourself, "I lived through this horror. I can take the next thing that comes along." . . . You must do the thing you think you cannot do.

You Learn by Living, pp. 29–30

Real education is knowledge that is not acquired from books alone.

Ladies' Home Journal, January 1942

We all create the person we become by our choices as we go through life. In a very real sense, by the time we are adult, we are the sum total of the choices we have made.

You Learn by Living, p. 51

We should always try to recognize the actual worth of a human being as such and, where opportunities have not been present, make allowances and work toward a world where every individual may have the chance to develop his abilities to the greatest possible extent.

Ladies' Home Journal, June 1941

One's philosophy is not best expressed in words; it is expressed in the choices one makes.

You Learn by Living, p. vii

Religion to me is simply the conviction that all human beings must hold some belief in a power greater than themselves, and that whatever their religious belief may be, it must move them to live better in this world and to approach whatever the future holds with serenity.

Ladies' Home Journal, October 1941

Once your children are grown up and have children of their own, the problems are theirs, and the less the older generation interferes the better.

Ladies' Home Journal, January 1946

If you face life with a spirit of adventure and with courage, you will get more out of it than if you are timid and unimaginative.

McCall's, December 1952

I think censorship over books is foolish, because anything harmful will probably be above children's heads and they will not take it in. They will absorb only what they are able to understand.

McCall's, November 1960

Teachers are more important than anything except parents in the lives of children.

Ladies' Home Journal, September 1946

I have always regretted that in my own teen-age I had so much responsibility that I never knew what it was to be carefree. It is in those years that one acquires a real *joie de vivre,* and it is a pity to miss out on it.

McCall's, February 1953

Looks alone do not make one attractive. . . . If you cultivate your mind and your spirit, you can have charm, which is far more important than looks.

Ladies' Home Journal, January 1949

I have never given very deep thought to a philosophy of life, though I have a few ideas that I think are useful to me. One is that you do whatever comes your way to do as well as you can, and another is that you think as little as possible about yourself and as much as possible about other people and about things that are interesting. The third is that you get more joy out of giving joy to others and should put a good deal of thought into the happiness that you are able to give.

McCall's, September 1957

Appendix C ———————

Tributes to Eleanor Roosevelt

The following tributes to Eleanor Roosevelt were made at the time of her death on November 7, 1962.

The first lady of the world.

Harry S. Truman

Mrs. Roosevelt was a lady of fine courage and great devotion to her country.

Herbert Hoover

The life of a historic and beloved American lady has ended. All in the world with a heart will mourn her loss.

Jacob K. Javits

Like so many others, I have lost more than a beloved friend. I have lost an inspiration. She would rather light a candle than curse the darkness, and her glow has warmed the world.

Adlai E. Stevenson

Her most enduring monument will be the gratitude, respect and love with which her name will always be remembered.

Bernard M. Baruch

No woman of this generation and few in the annals of history have so well understood and articulated the yearnings of men and women for social justice.

Jawaharlal Nehru

Those who were personally acquainted with Eleanor Roosevelt will always have the best of memories of her.

Andrei A. Gromyko

If democracy had saints—and no other cause demands a greater selflessness, a greater devotion—Mrs. Roosevelt would be one. She proved her faith in action as saints do. And, her memory may restore a measure of it to her country.

Archibald MacLeish

Notes

CHAPTER I

1. Eleanor Roosevelt, *The Autobiography of Eleanor Roosevelt* (New York: Harper & Brothers, 1958), 10.

2. Ibid., 9.

3. Ibid.

4. Ibid., 9, 11.

5. Ibid., 7.

6. Ibid., 10.

7. Ibid., 18.

8. Ibid., 20.

9. Ibid., 24.

10. Ibid., 29.

11. Ibid., 29.

12. Ibid., 31.

13. Ibid., 33.

14. Ibid., 31.

15. Ibid., 32.

16. Ibid., 37.

17. Ibid., 18.

18. Ibid., 40.

19. Ibid., 40, 41.

20. Joseph Lash, *Eleanor and Franklin* (New York: W.W. Norton & Co., 1971), 110.

21. Roosevelt, *Autobiography,* 42.

22. Ibid., 49.

23. Ibid., 50.
24. Ibid., 41.

CHAPTER 2

1. Joseph Lash, *Eleanor and Franklin* (New York: W.W. Norton & Co., 1971), 147.
2. Eleanor Roosevelt, *The Autobiography of Eleanor Roosevelt* (New York: Harper & Brothers, 1958), 56.
3. Ibid., 62.
4. Ibid., 63.
5. Ibid., 168.
6. Lash, *Eleanor and Franklin,* 139.
7. Ibid., 168.
8. Ibid., 252.
9. Roosevelt, *Autobiography,* 67.
10. Ibid., 68.
11. Lash, *Eleanor and Franklin,* 226.
12. Ibid., 227.
13. James R. Kearny, *Anna Eleanor Roosevelt: The Evolution of a Reformer* (Boston: Houghton Mifflin Company, 1968), 255; *New York Times* obituary of Mrs. W. Rutherford, August 1, 1948.
14. Roosevelt, *Autobiography,* 137.
15. Ibid.
16. Ibid., 142.
17. Ibid.
18. Ibid., 118.
19. Ibid., 120.
20. Lash, *Eleanor and Franklin,* 311.
21. Roosevelt, *Autobiography,* 119.
22. Ibid., 121.
23. Letter to the author.
24. Roosevelt, *Autobiography,* 155.
25. Ibid., 158.
26. Ibid., 157–58.
27. Interview with Dorothy Rosenman, 1983.
28. Roosevelt, *Autobiography,* 163.

CHAPTER 3

1. Eleanor Roosevelt, *The Autobiography of Eleanor Roosevelt* (New York: Harper & Brothers, 1958), 159.
2. Ibid., 164.

3. Ibid., 164, 175.

4. Joseph Lash, *Eleanor and Franklin* (New York: W.W. Norton & Co., 1971), 361.

5. Sophia M. Robison, comp., *Refugees at Work* (New York: King's Crown Press, 1942), vi. The American Friends Service Committee's study, under the auspices of Columbia University, showed that a considerable group of refugees had transplanted skills to America and, instead of displacing Americans, were employed in new trades.

6. Roosevelt, *Autobiography*, 184.

7. Ibid., 177.

8. Ibid., 184.

9. Ibid.

10. Helen Gahagan Douglas, *The Eleanor Roosevelt We Remember* (New York: Hill and Wang, 1963), 19–21.

11. Bernard Asbell, ed., *Mother & Daughter: The Letters of Eleanor and Anna Roosevelt* (New York: Coward, McCann & Geoghegan, 1982), 61, 77, 101.

12. Roosevelt, *Autobiography*, 206.

13. Interview with Ann Wallin, April 1983.

14. Roosevelt, *Autobiography*, 214.

15. Lash, *Eleanor and Franklin*, 617, 632.

16. Roosevelt, *Autobiography*, 225, 227.

17. Asbell, *Mother & Daughter*, 140.

18. Roosevelt, *Autobiography*, 227.

19. Ibid., 235.

20. Stella K. Hershan, *A Woman of Quality* (New York: Crown Publishers, 1970), 81–82.

21. Story told to the author, June 1982.

22. Roosevelt, *Autobiography*, 250.

23. Story told to the author, June 1982.

24. Roosevelt, *Autobiography*, 247.

25. Ibid., 254.

26. Hershan, *Woman of Quality*, 162–64.

27. Lash, *Eleanor and Franklin*, 687.

28. Roosevelt, *Autobiography*, 255.

29. Ibid., 262.

30. Ibid., 267.

31. Ibid., 269.

32. Mrs. Roosevelt leased the apartment in 1942 with the idea that she and the president would use it after leaving the White House. Eleanor first occupied the apartment full-time after her husband's death in 1945 and remained a Greenwich Village resident until 1949, when she moved to Val-Kill. In her book *This I Remember* (New York: Harper & Brothers, 1958, p. 272), she wrote: "We ended up at the apartment, which I had been trying to get Franklin to look

at. . . . He had told me to get an apartment in New York City specifying that it should be a place where he could work in peace and quiet, with no steps anywhere. He had every intention of spending the rest of his life, after leaving the White House, in Hyde Park and Warm Springs, but realized since he planned to do some magazine work that he must have some place in which to stay in New York City. He said that he liked the apartment very much" (*The Villager,* Oct. 2, 1986).

Though the apartment never became a residence for President Roosevelt, Eleanor loved the Village and spent seven busy years there. In 1985, two Greenwich Village residents started a drive to erect a plaque honoring Eleanor Roosevelt on the building at 29 Washington Square West, which by then belonged to New York University. With the help of James Roosevelt and John Brademas, president of NYU, the plan was approved and the plaque was dedicated on September 23, 1986.

33. Roosevelt, *Autobiography,* 264.

34. Ibid., 271.

35. William D. Hassett, *Off the Record with FDR, 1942–1945* (London: Ruskin House, George Allen & Unwin Ltd., 1960), 334n.

36. Joseph P. Lash, *The Years Alone* (New York: W. W. Norton & Company, 1972), 24.

CHAPTER 4

1. Eleanor Roosevelt, *The Autobiography of Eleanor Roosevelt* (New York: Harper & Brothers, 1958), 276.

2. When the Episcopal bishop of Washington in the first year of the Roosevelt administration asked the president to come to the National Cathedral for a special service of intercession, the president agreed. At the end of the service the bishop, as is customary, came to the portal to greet the president and wish him well. Roosevelt stopped to have a brief chat with him and the bishop walked out to his car beside him. He reminded Roosevelt that President Wilson was buried in the crypt and suggested that he at once make out a memorandum that he too wished to be buried there. On the way home, FDR muttered to his secretary, "The old body snatcher, the old body snatcher." That evening he dictated a memorandum to his heirs and assignees directing them that under no circumstances should his body be buried in the National Cathedral or any other cathedral but should lie peacefully in the ground at Hyde Park. Frances Perkins, *The Roosevelt I Knew* (New York: Viking Press, 1946), 145–46.

After the president's death, Eleanor Roosevelt handed her son James a sealed envelope which had been found in his father's safe and addressed to him in FDR's own hand. It was a four-page, handwritten document dated December 26, 1937. It gave specific instructions on every detail of how he wanted his funeral conducted in the event of his death while still president of the United

States. He directed that the casket be of absolute simplicity, dark wood, that the body should not be embalmed, and "that a plain white marble monument, no carving or decoration be placed over the grave." Franklin Roosevelt also wrote, "It is my hope that my dear wife will on her death be buried there also, and that the monument contain no device or inscription except the following on the South side:

Franklin Delano Roosevelt

1882–19–

Anna Eleanor Roosevelt

1884–19–"

Elliott Roosevelt and Sidney Shalett, eds., *Affectionately, F.D.R.: A Son's Story of a Courageous Man* (London: George G. Harrap, 1960), 328–30.

   3. Roosevelt, *Autobiography*, 287.

   4. Ibid., 279.

   5. Stella K. Hershan, *A Woman of Quality* (New York: Crown Publishers, 1970), 52.

   6. Ibid., 235.

   7. Bernard Asbell, ed., *Mother & Daughter: The Letters of Eleanor and Anna Roosevelt* (New York: Coward, McCann & Geoghegan, 1982), 203.

   8. Roosevelt, *Autobiography*, 301.

   9. Hershan, *Woman of Quality*, 245–46.

  10. Roosevelt, *Autobiography*, 305.

  11. Interview with Alexandra Holubowich, 1983.

  12. Roosevelt, *Autobiography*, 308.

  13. Ibid., 308.

  14. Ibid.

  15. Interview with James Frederick Green, 1982.

  16. Hershan, *Woman of Quality*, 73.

  17. Roosevelt, *Autobiography*, 333.

  18. Ibid., 323.

  19. Interview with Nancy Dubner, 1983.

  20. Interview with Roma Stibravy, 1983.

  21. Roosevelt, *Autobiography*, 340.

  22. Ibid.

  23. Hershan, *Woman of Quality*, 73–74.

  24. Interview with Maureen Corr, 1968.

  25. Hershan, *Woman of Quality*, 73.

  26. Roosevelt, *Autobiography*, 416.

  27. Asbell, *Mother & Daughter*, 312.

  28. Hershan, *Woman of Quality*, 31.

  29. Letter to the author, September 13, 1968.

  30. Eleanor Roosevelt, *You Learn by Living* (New York: Harper & Row, 1960), 100.

31. Gore Vidal, *New York Review of Books,* November 18, 1971.
32. Roosevelt, *Autobiography,* 436.
33. Letter to the author from Edward I. Koch, January 26, 1983.
34. Eulogy by Adlai Stevenson in "Memorial Addresses in the House of Representatives Together with Tributes on the Life of Anna Eleanor Roosevelt," Eighty-eighth Congress, First Session, 99–100.

CHAPTER 5

1. Interview with Frank and Rose Landolfa, January 1983.
2. Stella K. Hershan, *A Woman of Quality* (New York: Crown Publishers, 1970), 27.
3. Christmas List, Val-Kill.
4. Pamphlet, U.S. Department of the Interior, National Park Service, Eleanor Roosevelt National Historic Site.
5. Hershan, *Woman of Quality,* 214.
6. Interview with Nancy Dubner, March 1983.
7. *Hyde Park Townsman,* October 14, 1981, 2.
8. Interview with Emily Wright, September 1980.
9. Interview with Franceska Macsali, November 1992.

CHAPTER 6

1. Eleanor Roosevelt, *The Autobiography of Eleanor Roosevelt* (New York: Harper & Brothers, 1958), 285, and Clara and Hardy Steelholm, *The House at Hyde Park* (New York: Viking Press, 1950), 3.
2. Interview with Harold Nelson, August 1980.
3. Interview with Bill Hubbard, July 1982.
4. Story told to the author.
5. Interview with Haywood Smith, October 1984.
6. Emily Wright, "Fire Damages FDR's Hyde Park Home," *OAH Newsletter* vol. 10, no. 2, May 1982.

CHAPTER 7

1. "Out of Death, A Zest for Life," *New York Times,* November 15, 1982.
2. Letter to the author, November 1983. Dr. Perl died in Israel on November 24, 1988.
3. "Out of Death."
4. Interview with Mary C., June 1983.
5. Interview with Dutch journalist Jules Huf, April 1983.
6. Eleanor Roosevelt, "My Day," *New York Post,* April 22, 1952.

7. Eleanor Roosevelt, Introduction, in Anne Frank, *Anne Frank: Diary of a Young Girl* (New York: Doubleday & Co., 1952), vii–viii.

8. Letter to Eleanor Roosevelt from Otto Frank, March 25, 1952.

9. Interview with Jules Huf, April 1983.

10. Stella K. Hershan, "Exile and the Writer," in Martin Tucker, ed., *Exile and the Writer: A Special Confrontation Issue* (Greenvale, N.Y.: Long Island University Press, 1984), 127–129.

11. Marta Feuchtwanger, *Nurine Frau* (München, Germany: Langen Müller, 1983), 297.

12. Letter from Marta Feuchtwanger to Eleanor Roosevelt.

13. Letter from Eleanor Roosevelt to Marta Feuchtwanger, May 23, 1960.

CHAPTER 8

1. These letters are among the many addressed to the Performing Art Repertory Theater (PART) after the showing of the musical play *First Lady.*

2. Letter to the author, May 1983.

3. *Lakeville Journal* (Connecticut), August 28, 1952, 12.

4. *Choate News* (Wallingford, Conn.), May 11, 1940, 1.

CHAPTER 9

1. Letter to the author, September 30, 1983.

2. Excerpts from "Tribute to Eleanor Roosevelt" by Mrs. Lyndon B. Johnson. White House Press Release, April 9, 1964.

3. Eleanor Roosevelt, *The Autobiography of Eleanor Roosevelt* (New York: Harper & Brothers, 1958), 271.

4. Joseph Lash, *Eleanor and Franklin* (New York: W. W. Norton & Co., 1971), 252.

5. Letter to the author from Robert M. Morgenthau, December 28, 1989. Proceeds from a lecture conducted by Eleanor Roosevelt were contributed to the United Jewish Appeal in honor of Mrs. Henry Morgenthau, Jr. (Zionist Archives, 515 Park Ave., S., New York, N.Y., November 6, 1949).

6. Interview with Robert M. Morgenthau, December 1989.

7. The anonymous stories narrated in the following section were told to the author over a period of years.

8. Letter to the author, September 1983.

9. Letter to the author, September 1983.

10. Letter to the author from Anna M. McKnight, May 18, 1982; letter to the author from Maxwell S. McKnight, May 31, 1982; and J. Gansberg, *Stalag U.S.A.: The Remarkable Story of German POWs in America* (New York: Thomas Y. Crowell Co., 1977), 61–64.

11. Letter to the author from Dr. Hans Hannau, February 1980.

12. Interview with Jack Greenway, February 1983.

13. Interview with Mary Jeffries, February 1983.

14. Interview with Dorothy Rosenman, June 1983.

15. Stella K. Hershan, *A Woman of Quality* (New York: Crown Publishers, 1970), 99–101.

16. Interview with W. Colston Leigh, June 1983.

17. Story told to the author by Donald Cummings, November 1992.

18. Interview with Maureen Corr.

19. Letter to the author from Herbert Zohn.

CHAPTER 10

1. Interview with the Reverend Gordon L. Kidd.

2. *New York Times,* November 11, 1962.

Selected Bibliography

Asbell, Bernard, ed. *Mother & Daughter: The Letters of Eleanor and Anna Roosevelt.* New York: Coward, McCann & Geoghegan, 1982.

Douglas, Helen Gahagan. *The Eleanor Roosevelt We Remember.* New York: Hill and Wang, 1963.

Frank, Anne. *Anne Frank: The Diary of a Young Girl.* Introduction by Eleanor Roosevelt. New York: Doubleday & Co., 1952.

Gurewitsch, A. David. *Eleanor Roosevelt: Her Day; A Personal Album.* New York: Quadrangle, 1974.

Hershan, Stella K. *A Woman of Quality.* New York: Crown Publishers, 1970.

Hoff-Wilson, Joan, and Marjorie Lightman, eds. *Without Precedent: The Life and Career of Eleanor Roosevelt.* Bloomington: Indiana University Press, 1984.

Lash, Joseph. *Eleanor: The Years Alone.* New York: W.W. Norton & Co., 1972.

———. *Eleanor and Franklin.* New York: W.W. Norton & Co., 1971.

———. *Eleanor Roosevelt: A Friend's Memoir.* New York: Doubleday & Co., 1964.

———. *Life Was Meant to Be Lived.* New York: W.W. Norton & Co., 1984.

———. *Love, Eleanor.* New York: Doubleday & Co., 1982.

MacLeish, Archibald. *The Eleanor Roosevelt Story.* Boston: Houghton Mifflin & Co., 1965.

Memorial Address in the House of Representatives Together with Tributes on the Life and Ideals of Anna Eleanor Roosevelt. 88th Congress, First Session. House Resolution No. 343. March 18, 1963.

Perkins, Frances. *The Roosevelt I Knew.* New York: Viking Press, 1946.

Robison, Sophia M., comp. *Refugees at Work.* New York: King's Crown Press, 1942.

Roosevelt, Eleanor. *The Autobiography of Eleanor Roosevelt.* New York: Harper & Brothers, 1958.

————. *On My Own: The Years since the White House.* New York: Harper & Brothers, 1958.

————. *This Is My Story.* New York: Harper & Brothers, 1937.

————. *You Learn by Living.* New York: Harper & Row, 1960.

Roosevelt, Elliot. *Eleanor Roosevelt, With Love: A Centenary Remembrance.* New York: E. P. Dutton, 1984.

Roosevelt, James and Sidney Shallett, eds. *Affectionately, F.D.R.: A Son's Story of a Courageous Man.* London: George G. Harrap, 1960.

Steelholm, Clara and Hardy. *The House at Hyde Park.* New York: Viking Press, 1950.

Steinberg, Alfred. *Mrs. R.: The Life of Eleanor Roosevelt.* New York: G. P. Putnam & Sons, 1958.

Tucker, Martin, ed. *Exile and the Writer: A Special Confrontation Issue.* Greenvale, N.Y.: Long Island University Press, 1984.

Whitney, Sharon. *Eleanor Roosevelt.* New York: Franklin Watts, 1982.

Index

Eleanor Roosevelt Maquette

A Woman of Quality

The Candles She Lit

Cookbook

PBS Video

Stamp Pin

Tote Bag

Ceramic Mug

Sweat/Tee Shirt

Blank Note Cards

Blue Book Mark

Purple Book Mark

Gift Store Items

Eleanor Roosevelt Monument Maquette: ERVK is the exclusive distributor for the beautiful and unique Eleanor Roosevelt Monument Maquette. The 14" bonded bronze sculpture by Penelope Jencks is a replica of the 8 foot monument in New York City. This beautiful artwork has been used as an inspiring organizational award and as a special personal gift. Each Maquette is $250 plus $15s/h

ERVK Publications

A Woman of Quality - By Stella K. Hershan. First published in 1970, and previously out of print, now made available and published by the Eleanor Roosevelt Center at Val-Kill. A fitting tribute to Eleanor Roosevelt. This is a collection of anecdotes, stories and memories about Eleanor Roosevelt. $15.00 plus $4.00s/h

The Candles She Lit - By Stella K. Hershan. First published in 1993 and previously out of print, now made available and published by the Eleanor Roosevelt Center at Val-Kill. This is both a brief biography of Eleanor Roosevelt and a testimony to the positive and influential effect she had on others. $15.00 plus $4.00s/h

Ms. Hershan's books can be purchased as a set for $25.00 plus 5.00s/h

The Val Kill Cookbook - A popular collection of recipes and photos (including holiday and entertaining ideas) from Roosevelt family and friends. $9.95 plus $4s/h

Novelty Items

Eleanor Roosevelt - An American Experience - PBS Home Video - 150 Minutes on the life of America's Most Powerful Woman. $19.95 plus $4s/h

Eleanor Roosevelt Stamp Pin - Mrs. Roosevelt smiles from this lovely laminated lapel stamp pin. Wear with pride. $6.00 plus $2s/h

Eleanor Roosevelt Tote Bag - Beautifully designed tote with picture of Eleanor Roosevelt on front with quote: "The Future Belongs to Those Who Believe in the Beauty of Their Dreams" On back: illustration of Stone Cottage by artist: Elayne Seaman. $15.00 plus $2s/h

Mug - This 12oz two tone mug in white ceramic with dark blue handle and rim features Eleanor Roosevelt at 15 years of age on front. "The Future Belongs to Those Who Believe in the Beauty of Their Dreams" on back. Print in dark blue. $8.00 plus $4s/h

Sweatshirt - Beige sweatshirt with dark blue Eleanor Roosevelt picture and quote: "The Future Belongs to Those Who Believe in the Beauty of Their Dreams" $25 plus $4s/h Sizes: S, M, L, XL, XXL - Children's -white only Sizes S, M, L

Tee Shirt - White 100% cotton tee with dark blue Eleanor Roosevelt photo/quote: "The Future Belongs to Those Who Believe in the Beauty of Their Dreams" $15 plus $4s/h Sizes: S, M, L. XL, XXL - Children's Sizes S, M, L

Note Cards (Blank) - Beautiful Stone Cottage line drawing by artist Elayne Seaman is printed on heavy ecru paper. Set is package of five (incl. envelopes). $6.00 plus $2s/h

Eleanor Roosevelt Stamp Bookmark - Laminated Bookmark w/ U.S. issue Postage Stamp, beautifully decorated with Eleanor Roosevelt quote. Blue bookmark quote: "The Future Belongs to Those Who Believe in the Beauty of Their Dreams" Purple bookmark quote: "No One Can Make You Feel Inferior Without Your Consent" $4 plus $1s/h

Please send this order form with your payment to:

ERVK, PO Box 255, Hyde Park, New York 12538

Name:_____

Address :_____Apt:_____

City:_____ State:_____ Zip:_____

Daytime phone:(___)_____ E: Mail:_____

Ship to: (if different from above) (UPS will not deliver to a P.O. Box)

Name_____

Address: _____Apt: _____

City:_____ State:_____ Zip:_____

ERVK does not accept C.O.D. deliveries.

Please make checks payable to: ERVK

We accept all major credit cards

If paying by credit card, please fill out order form below:

Credit Card #_____/_____/_____/_____

Expiration Date: _____

Item	Price	Quantity	Total
Shipping/Handling			
NYS Sales Tax 7.25%			
Total			

Please send this order form with your payment to:

ERVK, PO Box 255, Hyde Park, New York 12538

Name:_____

Address :_____Apt:_____

City:_____ State:_____ Zip:_____

Daytime phone:(___)_____ E: Mail:_____

Ship to: (if different from above) (UPS will not deliver to a P.O. Box)

Name_____

Address: _____Apt: _____

City:_____ State:_____ Zip:_____

ERVK does not accept C.O.D. deliveries.

Please make checks payable to: ERVK

We accept all major credit cards

If paying by credit card, please fill out order form below:

Credit Card #_____/____._____/_____/_____

Expiration Date: _____

Item	Price	Quantity	Total
Shipping/Handling			
NYS Sales Tax 7.25%			
Total			

Please send this order form with your payment to:

ERVK, PO Box 255, Hyde Park, New York 12538

Name:_____

Address :_____Apt:_____

City:_____ State:_____ Zip:_____

Daytime phone:(___)_____ E: Mail:_____

Ship to: (if different from above) (UPS will not deliver to a P.O. Box)

Name_____

Address: _____Apt: _____

City:_____ State:_____ Zip:_____

ERVK does not accept C.O.D. deliveries.

Please make checks payable to: ERVK

We accept all major credit cards

If paying by credit card, please fill out order form below:

Credit Card #_____/_____/_____/_____

Expiration Date: _____

Item	Price	Quantity	Total
Shipping/Handling			
NYS Sales Tax 7.25%			
Total			

Please send this order form with your payment to:

ERVK, PO Box 255, Hyde Park, New York 12538

Name:_____

Address :_____Apt:_____

City:_____ State:_____ Zip:_____

Daytime phone:(___)_____ E: Mail:_____

Ship to: (if different from above) (UPS will not deliver to a P.O. Box)

Name_____

Address: _____Apt: _____

City:_____ State:_____ Zip:_____

ERVK does not accept C.O.D. deliveries.

Please make checks payable to: ERVK

We accept all major credit cards

If paying by credit card, please fill out order form below:

Credit Card #_____/_____/_____/_____

Expiration Date: _____

Item	Price	Quantity	Total
Shipping/Handling			
NYS Sales Tax 7.25%			
Total			

Please send this order form with your payment to:

ERVK, PO Box 255, Hyde Park, New York 12538

Name:_____

Address :_____Apt:_____

City:_____ State:_____ Zip:_____

Daytime phone:(___)_____ E: Mail:_____

Ship to: (if different from above) (UPS will not deliver to a P.O. Box)

Name_____

Address: _____Apt: _____

City:_____ State:_____ Zip:_____

ERVK does not accept C.O.D. deliveries.

Please make checks payable to: ERVK

We accept all major credit cards

If paying by credit card, please fill out order form below:

Credit Card #_____/_____/_____/_____

Expiration Date: _____

Item	Price	Quantity	Total
Shipping/Handling			
NYS Sales Tax 7.25%			
Total			